WALKING IN THE SHADOW OF DEATH

The Story of a Vietnam Infantry Soldier

WILLIAM HENDERSON

ISBN 978-1-64003-173-9 (Paperback)
ISBN 978-1-64003-174-6 (Digital)

Covenant Books, Inc.
11661 Hwy 707
Murrells Inlet, SC 29576
www.covenantbooks.com

I wish to dedicate this work to my late wife, Judy Henderson, who encouraged me to write my story, even as I struggled at the many attempts to write. She was with me at our two reunions and later recalled how amazed she was at this group of men who were together so long ago; that they could rekindle their friendships like never having parted. Judy succumbed to cancer in 2011.

Some would say that I am an old man. I wonder, *When did that happen?* If it is true, I want to tell my story before it is too late! There has been much written and said over the years about the war in Southeast Asia. Unfortunately, much of what I have read gives an unfair picture of the Vietnam soldier. If you will notice the stories written about Vietnam before 9/11, many of the accounts were condemning to those who served. All we wanted to do was to stay alive by protecting each other. I did not see the depravity, which at times was tagged upon US soldiers by the writers and movie producers, eager to sell their story. It was an unpopular war, and as such, people were quick to criticize those of us who participated.

Because so much of this story has affected my life, I want it to be known to my children, my siblings, and my grandchildren. Anyone else inclined to read this account is welcome to do so. I also realize I open myself to criticism for my part in this war. The events may not be in correct chronological order but are recorded according to my personal reflections more than forty-five years later. I do understand the perceptions I have of an incident may be somewhat different to one who experienced the same incident. I say this because I will encourage my fellow comrades to read this account. I will welcome comments from them.

When I returned from Vietnam in 1971, my mother gave to me all the letters that I had written to the family during the year. I did a very foolish thing. I took them out to the burn barrel and lit them afire. In that fire went all the emotion and accounts of the past years. No more record of my absence, no personal thoughts during my days in the military, no history to give to my wife, my children, grandchildren, or siblings. I have agonized about this for the past forty-five years.

This is my story.

The night is quiet. Darkness comes early in the jungle of giant hardwood trees. We are on high ground under the canopy. The birds and creatures of the area have found their secure areas for the evening. It is very quiet! The men of Second Platoon have divided up into groups of three or four and are positioned into a perimeter setting. The first watch is to be awake in each position. We take turns awakening each other every two hours or so depending upon how many are in the night position. I am on the perimeter with my ever-present RTO (radio operator). The two of us are inseparable; he tags along by my side day and night. Sometimes I get pissed at him because he is not quiet in his position. Sometimes he gets frustrated with me as I constantly ask about radio frequencies, battery life of the radio, and security issues. I don't think he fully realizes the connection of the pack on his back to the safety of all of us.

He told me his name was Barney. "Call me Barney Bad-ass." Those were his words on our first meeting when he joined us for the tour. Barney had that guttural laugh when he was feeling friendly. "There it is," he would say with that evil-sounding laugh. Eventually Barney fell into the world where many of the Blacks hung out in the rear area. Barney is white. I was afraid we were losing Barney to that culture.

I'm lying on my back on the jungle floor. I turn to lie sideways, but my hip gets sore from the ground. I did not take time before darkness to scoop out a small depression for my hips. I lie there, knowing my first watch will come soon. I must sleep. It is 9:00 p.m., and my first watch is 1:00–2:00 a.m. Just before darkness, I walked to each position, approaching from the backside (inner circle), checking one last time that everyone who was supposed to be on guard was alert. "Who's on guard?" I would whisper into the group. If I did not hear a response, I woke everyone, and that *one* received a quiet but firm tongue-lashing. It had been a hard day. We humped several "klicks" (kilometers) before getting into our NDP (night defensive position). I learned early in my tour that fatigue always trumped fear. You could be very fearful of the night but sleep would consume you if you had not properly rested.

I always took the last watch, 1:00–2:00 a.m. and 5:00–6:00 a.m. It was always the most dangerous time for us—in the morning. The enemy would crawl quietly during the night to reach within yards of our position. That would be a devastating surprise to us in the morning first light. It was at first light that we were most vulnerable. If someone had fallen asleep and did not wake the next person for watch, the entire position would be asleep during this most crucial time. If the enemy successfully penetrated our perimeter, it would be devastating to all of us. If no one attempted to wake me at 5:00 a.m. (before first light), someone had slept through his watch. Fortunately, my inner clock always seemed to alert me near first light.

First light meant sitting up from the ground, if you were behind the foxhole, listening for movement outside the perimeter, cautiously rising to stretch one's legs, stepping back into the perimeter to urinate. Not a good time to have a bowel movement; that could wait for another time. Besides you want to do that outside the perimeter.

Picture a small hole, "foxhole," large enough for one person. That was the guard position. Others in the position sprawled out behind the hole. When it was your turn, the on-guard person tapped you on your foot and you exchanged positions. Most often the hole was only large enough for one person. At times we dug a large fighting position depending upon what we had encountered during the day and what we expected during the night. Each day we moved a few klicks to another NDP. We never stayed in the same position more than one night.

Tonight I am finally settled in. I say the prayers that always made me feel secure, the Our Father, the Apostle's Creed, Psalm 23 and then asking for wisdom and knowledge to make the right decisions in the time ahead. I pray for the security for those to whom I am responsible. I pray for my family back home, that they will be safe, and if it is his will, that I too will return alive. In the beginning days of my tour, I was much concerned with my personal safety. As I undertook the responsibility placed upon me, my request to the Lord was that he guide me in my actions and decisions so that harm to others will not occur under my responsibility. "Lord, keep us all safe." Tonight I am at peace knowing that I am heard.

I reflect, "How did I get into this situation?" I try not to dwell on it, as I fully understand how this occurred. Early in life, I always knew that I would join the military. My brothers had gone before me. I was filled with patriotic duty, to go wherever my country called. This war started when I was a college student. Every day I watched the news about events in Southeast Asia. I too would be there eventually. The thought of being in Vietnam did not frighten me. It was to be! I could not plan any long-term relationship with a woman. Certainly there were many eligible throughout my college career and including the year I spent working as a schoolteacher in western North Dakota. College, military, and marriage were my early goals, and it was to be in that order!

Bowman, North Dakota, is where I had to report to be transported to Fargo to be inducted. A member of the selective service board from Bowman County was required to drive me to Dickinson to board a bus so that I could report to the Induction Center in Fargo. From Fargo, we would ride the train to Fort Lewis, Washington, to begin army basic training. When my mother woke me, it was very early in the morning. As we entered the family auto, she said, "You rest, I'll drive." During the twelve-mile ride to Bowman, I couldn't help but see the anguish on her face as we rode in silence. The war in Vietnam was still raging with daily body counts. As I looked upon that motherly face, I could not stop feeling guilty having to put her through this ordeal one more time. Previously, two brothers made the same journey to Bowman.

As I waited to board the bus in Dickinson, I noted several other young men apparently in my position going off to the military. I saw their family members giving final good-byes, some crying as they clung to each other. We boarded and stopped at most small towns along Highway 10 going east. Other young men boarded at various stops. Soon the bus was nearly full except for a few seats in the far back. It was quiet on board. At one stop a middle-aged woman got on the bus and stood for a short time assessing where to sit. I observed that no one in front of me gave up his seat for the lady. Since I was near the front, I stood and indicated that she could have my seat. The bus driver noted the mannerly act for the lady. As I walked to the back of the bus, I heard the driver speak out for all on board to hear, "Someday that man will make a good officer!"

I did not think that basic training was that difficult. I observed what others were doing and how they responded to authority and to conditioning. North Dakota inductees numbered about twenty. The rest of the barracks of about thirty troops were from the Seattle area. They were on average younger than the North Dakota boys. In fact, most were just out of high school, and they were enlisted men starting their three-year commitment while the rest of us were draftees in for two years. We had some minor issues with the young men over time. At least one young man thought his intelligence was superior to everyone else.

He was quite naïve. He told us his MOS (military occupation service) was going to be working with intelligence. The army guaranteed this assignment when he enlisted.

One Sunday afternoon, four of us were playing cards in the barracks. We were bantering back and forth, ribbing each other about MOS assignments about to be handed out in the future. One of the guys called the MOS assignments "masturbation papers." At that time, the young troop from Seattle who was going into intelligence was walking by the card game. He stopped to observe and listen, thinking he might have missed out on something. The army is always full of rumors that everyone needs to hear! Paul McKinnon said to me, "Hey, Bill, have you received your masturbation papers?"

"Yes, I did. Got mine yesterday," I replied, noting the young man was still listening. The others spoke up indicating they had theirs also as they immediately picked up on the ruse. Now this was very upsetting to the Seattle troop! He wanted to know where to get the masturbation papers, as he had not received his yet.

I think it was Paul who said to "Seattle," "You better get right over to the orderly room and pick them up. I'm surprised you don't have them. All the rest of us have ours." We all chimed in agreeing with Paul attempting to keep sober faces and trying to continue the card game as this conversation was going on.

"Okay, I'm going right now to get mine. You say you got them from the captain at the orderly room?" questioned Seattle. We all agreed that this was the place and time to get the papers. Seattle dashed out of the barracks while the rest of us ran to the windows to observe what was about to happen.

"He is really going to do it!" We were howling with laughter not believing what we were about to witness. We observe Seattle as he knocks on the orderly room door. The captain comes to the doorway, Seattle salutes the officer, and a conversation occurs, but we are unable to hear. Then we see Seattle saluting again, indicating the conversation has ended. The captain returns the salute. Seattle turns and runs back into the barracks.

"The captain wants everyone to fall out right now," shouts Seattle.

"Oh no, we're all in trouble now" is what everyone is thinking. We line up in formation out in front of the barracks and wait for the captain to emerge from the orderly room.

Donovan Thole is standing next to me, and I whisper to him, "This is going to be push-up time!"

We are standing there for a full minute before the captain emerges and begins his swagger toward the formation. He addresses the group. "Get on down! Now!" We drop on our bellies. "It appears we have lost Seattle's masturbation papers. We believe the papers are somewhere on the parade grounds. Start crawling until you find those papers!" With that said, the captain turns and rapidly walks toward the orderly room snorting, trying to contain his laughter as we are lying on the ground laughing and howling.

Basic training is over. I report to the orderly room to receive papers revealing my job assignment. I salute the company commander and extend my hand to accept the papers. The captain watches my reaction as I read the number 11B. *Infantry!* My fate is sealed. I am a ground pounder with the future being Vietnam. "Men are dying in Vietnam!" Even though I knew it was going to happen, I was shocked. Before I had volunteered for the draft, friends kept telling me that I would not be assigned infantry because I was a college graduate. Even then I had mixed feelings about their comments. As I salute the captain to leave, he replies, "We need good men in the infantry. Congratulations!" Was it my education that rewarded me with this "death ending" infantry 11B status? Was it because I was twenty-four years old, older than most everyone in the company of 150? How could I be given this assignment? Just two days before, I was recognized at graduation ceremonies as the outstanding basic training recruit. Did they not send the blind to lead the blind? When I returned to the barracks, it seemed I was the only one assigned 11B. All others were celebrating their assignments, so it seemed.

After basic training, 11B infantry were sent across base at Fort Lewis, Washington, to the next phase called AIT (advanced infantry training), which was light-weapons training for a duration of eight weeks. It was during this phase that the average infantry soldier received weapons training on all that was to be available during combat for that grade of soldier. Next stop, the Republic of South Vietnam. So I thought.

I was called out from group formation after the eighth week of AIT. "PFC [private first class] Henderson is ordered to report to Fort Benning, GA, upon completion of AIT." Now what's happening? As it turns out, the casualties of war had taken its toll on the noncommissioned officer ranks. Additional trained squad leaders were required for the war effort. What the heck! I am guaranteed an additional twenty weeks stateside before going across to the war zone. Do I want to do this? I have an opportunity to reject the order after reporting to Fort Benning. I could make the decision then to forego the NCO school (noncommission officer school), and my orders would be changed, sending me immediately to Vietnam.

The reality is, if I elect not to complete the school at Benning, I will be sent overseas as a private and no leadership responsibility. If I do successfully complete the program, I will have the rank of sergeant E-5 and will be expected to become a squad leader when joining my unit in Vietnam. Do I want that responsibility? Twenty additional weeks stateside sounded quite attractive at the moment. "I'll do it!"

After the twelfth week of NCO school in Georgia, our final training session was a twelve-mile march to an unknown location. Once we arrived at the destination, we rested, ate a small lunch, and prepared to walk back. As we readied our gear, a military jeep pulled up in front of the formation. An impressive-looking soldier with sharply creased combat fatigues stepped out to address us. "You owe it to yourself and to the men in Vietnam to acquire the best possible training. The next step for you to get that training is to come with me, and I will take you to the Ranger Training Headquarters back at base camp." Much more was said, but I remember the words, "You owe it to yourself. You owe it to your fellow men to have the best training." And then, he enticed us with, "Jump in the jeep, and I'll give you a ride back to camp." Not sure what I should do, hesitating and yet willing to step forward at same time, I looked at Candidate Hines, my close buddy at the school.

He returned my look and said quite emphatically, "I don't know about you, but I'm not walking back." So it was that we were off to ranger training. Leon Haxton (Haxton, Henderson, Hines close bunkmates) also committed that day. Could we survive the training and be awarded the coveted tab? Those who successfully completed the course proudly wore the orange ranger tab upon their left shoulder. I came to believe that this event was about to become the proudest moment of my life.

Nine weeks later, I stood on the graduation platform to receive the coveted tab. With the ranger training behind, I felt more confident in what I would have to deal with in Vietnam. The training emphasized "leading successful patrols," physical conditioning, and understanding your own capability under extreme conditions. The irony of this successful step was the additional rank. I was now a staff sergeant E-6. This rank called for more responsibility. I was now expected to become a platoon sergeant immediately upon joining my unit assignment in Vietnam. A fact about the military, as you increase in rank, they expect more from you in leadership and responsibility. Little did I know that my first leadership position in Vietnam was not to be a platoon sergeant but to become a platoon leader, a position usually held by a commissioned officer, a second lieutenant!

The army allowed me to go home for ten days before I had to report to Fort Lewis, Washington, for the overseas flight to Vietnam. I had a great time those days. I lived that time like they were the last days of my life. My mind was clear; my mission was set before me. I trusted that the God I knew had a plan, and I was prepared to accept that plan without question. My concern was with my mother who was deeply troubled. Someone had to drive me to Bismarck to meet my flight. It would not be my mother. I hugged her standing on Main Street in Scranton, saying my good-bye. Her tear tore my heart apart. She was such a strong woman. Previously, two other sons left in like manner.

Earlier two friends, Les Schaefer and Harry Hirsch, made plans to drive me to Bismarck. We bantered and joked all the way, keeping the conversation light. Arriving two hours before flight time, I checked in, and the three of us headed toward the airport lounge. (This was before airport security 9/11.) We had a drink. We had a second drink. An announcement was made that the flight leaving for Seattle, Washington, would be late. Our conversation was animated. Les would get my golf clubs if I did not return. And it went on as such until Les jumped up and said, "It's only fitting that a good-looking girl should be here to send you off to war. I'll be right back."

Sure enough! Les returned with a beautiful young lady, as he had announced earlier. Introductions were made. This gamely young lovely woman sat with us until my flight was called. As in a scripted rehearsal, she walked with me to the gate and put her lips upon mine in a most friendly way. With that moment seared into my memory, I boarded the plane destined for Vietnam!

2

Everyone had to undergo one week of acclimation to Vietnam, which included adapting to the hot humid climate. My week of acclimation was at the 101st Airborne (Airmobile) Division reception center at Camp Eagle, South Vietnam. I had been assigned to the 101st Division presently located in I Corps in northern South Vietnam. The division assignment was to stop infiltration by the North Vietnamese into South Vietnam. From here, we were assigned to various units within the 101st area of operation. There was a one week of classes, which included information about the enemy. I was most intrigued with the demonstration of the sapper. A sapper is a special-trained North Vietnamese soldier whose skill was stealth and who had the expertise in making satchel charges (TNT explosives). Sappers were especially trained to move in the darkness of the night and infiltrate a nighttime defensive position (NDP). They could crawl undetected through the jungle underbrush all evening and be in a position to attack at first light. Upon breaching the perimeter, they were followed by others who would rake the NDP with automatic weapons fire, grenades, etc. A breach in the perimeter was not acceptable, and we were all aware of the consequences.

"Labruna!" I called out. "I need you, let's go." So it was that I unknowingly called upon this young man so many times in the heat of the moment just off hill 1000. In the valley below, the enemy was heavily entrenched. I had received the operations order the night before from the command post, indicating that C Company, Second Platoon would follow A Company off the hill in the morning to engage the enemy in the valley. We were told that the valley would be prepped with artillery and five-hundred-pound bombs from strafing jets before we descended below. Also, "Tell your men that they should not stop to pick souvenirs from the dead during your advance." This was it! Real life was about to unfold before me. Such were my thoughts as I returned to my platoon. I needed to give them a quick brief operations order relayed from the company commander. Problem was, everyone was dug in and hunkered down into their fighting positions, perhaps writing their final letters to friends, family, and sweethearts. There was no getting them out of their holes. We were all anxious and fearful to see what the morning light would bring. For at least seven of us in Second Platoon, this was our first operation into the forested, mountainous jungles of northern South Vietnam against a determined enemy.

I didn't sleep well that night. Again, "What the hell am I doing here? What did I get myself into?" Believe it or not, at times I felt this was my calling, to be here. I was scared but determined not to let it show. These men depended upon me as well upon the others. "Dear God, please don't let me fail in what lies ahead. No man should die because of me. I'm new to all this! I hardly know everybody's name" were my thoughts and prayers. Tonight there are fourteen of us in Second Platoon. Second platoon had previously walked into an ambush days before I arrived. The wounded and dead had been evacuated. A few that were wounded would return to the field weeks later.

It was this reason seven of us joined at the same time. I had one evening, about six hours, to meet my platoon of men for the first time. The entire company had returned to base camp. A short memorial service was held. I remember the chaplain saying some words and prayers, hoping to comfort the surviving members of the unit. After the service, I met in a tent with Second Platoon survivors and with the replacements. I introduced myself. It was somber. Those who had just returned were preoccupied with the terrible past events. Those of us who were new were occupied with questions about tomorrow. At first light, we were going back out to the same area of operation. "Is this for real? Lord, help me! Don't let me fail in this new responsibility!"

I needed help in preparation for what to expect. Two "old" members of the platoon stepped forward after my initial greeting. Sergeant Gayland Davis and Sergeant Jack Hammonds quickly briefed me on how the platoon had functioned, who the reliable troops were, and hinted about which ones I could not depend upon to be effective. Unfortunately, the surviving platoon sergeant was one that was deemed ineffective. I needed him to brief me. I needed him to step up and be a leader. Now I am a platoon leader with an ineffective platoon sergeant who is nowhere to be seen! He dashed to a remote corner of the compound to smoke some weed right after the memorial service. *Damn!* No lieutenant, no platoon sergeant, six new "cherries," and tomorrow we go right back out to battle in the same AO (area operation).

So much to do in so little time! We are scheduled to CA (combat assault) at first light. I have to make sure I have enough ammunition—one hundred rounds, two hundred rounds? What do I need? I am told my rucksack will be around seventy to eighty pounds once I have all that is needed. Two gallons water, c rations for one week, one claymore mine, bandages, six hand grenades, red and green smoke canisters, a briefing by the RTO (radio operator) who will be by my side constantly. I need to be briefed on the SOI passwords so that I can communicate with headquarters. "When will all this come together for me?" Tomorrow we board the choppers to make the assault. Destination, Firebase Ripcord at the edge of the Ashua Valley! We are needed to bring support to the men of the besieged firebase.

Morning came. Word filtered down that we have ten minutes to get to the helipad to board. As we waited for the helicopters, the chaplain said a prayer and prepared us for Holy Communion. It was the platoon sergeant's responsibility to manifest the loading. He stood behind the rucked-up soldiers, unwilling to direct the men to the choppers, unwilling to lead in any way. We were fourteen in number. We board six to seven per chopper.

As the birds came in to land, I saw that my sergeant did not make a move to indicate which bird each would be on. As platoon leader, I was to go in on the first chopper with six others. I pointed to the six and shouted to board. Before we jumped aboard, the chaplain gave communion and blessed each of us with the sign of the cross dispensing the host. As my ride lifted off, I wasn't sure how the others would board, but they did. I prayed that morning, before the flight, during the flight, and tried to convince myself, "What is to happen is now in God's hands." That was comforting!

I had ridden helicopters stateside in ranger training, but then we were seated with the doors closed on the choppers. Here there were no doors. Two soldiers sat in the center of the chopper behind the pilots, and two soldiers sat each side on the edge of the chopper floor-feet dangling, not even close to touching the helicopter skids! So we sat four combatants, feet dangling, fully rucked with sixty to eighty pounds on our backs. I placed my left hand along the edge of the fuselage near the feet of the helicopter door gunner. The two door gunners, left and right, operated the M-60 machine guns attached to the chopper. There were times as we came into a landing zone, the door gunners opened fire with their M-60s, prepping the area to drive the enemy back and to detonate any booby traps intended to do us harm. Truly deafening as I would sit next to the machine gun! The flight with my feet dangling, the sound of the helicopter, the deafening *rat-a-tat* of the machine guns and the intense excitement of the unknown created an adrenalin rush!

I remember the beauty of the ground below me. The vista was astoundingly beautiful! Rice paddies and the locals working the fields passed beneath. So many thoughts flooded my mind. "I hope I get an opportunity to enjoy this at a different time!" For now, I'm thinking this could be my first and last ride in Vietnam. "Lord, protect us as we enter into the area of combat!"

The first morning mission was like a cluster melee. "Will it always be like this?" My platoon sergeant had been described accurately by the previous night comments. We try to keep the squads together, but since I just pointed and said board, I wasn't sure that happened. When we dismount into the jungle, the squad leaders need to know where their members are.

Ralph Labuna, George Swantek, Steve Nyguard, Punky Stevenson, Larry Thosteson, Oscar Gonzales (Poncho), and others that I will name later became my family. We all came in together. This was their first mission also. Pray that we all return together. They wanted as much as I to remain alive, and I trusted they would perform their duties in a manner that one day we would all survive this ordeal.

Our tour was 365 days, and already fourteen of those days had passed! When we landed at Cam Rhan Bay in South Vietnam, we had just completed a twenty-one-hour flight from Fort Lewis, Washington. Two days in Cam Rhan Bay before our orders were to arrive. A blast of hot sticky humid air hit our faces as we stepped from the air-conditioned airplane. The air smelled like diesel fuel fires, as what was really happening! Human feces were being burned in containers filled with diesel fuel. Why? Because the ground water in the lowlands was near the soil surface. How could it burn? Someone had to stir it as the fuel burned the excrement. From Cam Rhan Bay, we shipped north to the 101st ABN airmobile division and entered P training at SERTS (screaming eagle replacement station). Here, we would become acclimated to the country and get to know the enemy. It was here that I first learned about the NVA sappers.

"Labruna!" It was this time I overheard him say, "What the hell, am I the only one he knows?" We needed to move off Hill 1000. A Company ran into machine gun bunkers in the valley below and they were taking heavy casualties. The advance was halted. Instead of following A Company off the hill to join in the attack, we were now needed to become litter and ammo carriers. We were needed to carry ammunition to the valley and to bring the wounded and dead back to the top of the hill to be airlifted out. When my orders came in to send men below, I ordered my platoon sergeant to give me five men to come with me. He turned away and sat in his hole. The fear was in his eyes; he wanted no more of this. He sat in his two-person hole with the first squad leader. He, also, refused to move. These were the two of three that the sergeants spoke about days before. I knew we would have to be rid of these two to become effective. Later had I pressed, they could have had court martial charges brought upon them.

I had one previous encounter with these two. It was the first night on an NDP position with them atop an adjacent hill from Hill 1000. I made my rounds to each fighting position. These two were in a foxhole to themselves. They were smoking grass. It was nearly dark, and they didn't seem inclined to conceal the glowing embers, nor did they care if a superior was in their presence. I made small talk with them. "Do you know what is in your field of fire? How far out did the terrain drop?" All this, as I was checking their reaction to my presence? The first squad leader spoke up, "Do you want a hit?"

"No," I replied, "but you need to know, this is the last time you will smoke pot in the field in this platoon." These were two experienced soldiers whom I thought I could count on to help the new troops, to set an example, to teach others the intricacies of surviving. No matter what your rank, you had to learn quickly from those who had been on the ground and had experience in the ways of the jungle warfare. I especially needed help from my platoon sergeant. He avoided me totally and would not look at me.

The next incident occurred weeks later. They had not smoked in the field that I knew of since our first encounter. One day as we waited on the trail sitting on our rucksacks, I heard guys talking. This was beyond what I would have expected from our soldiers in this army of men. We were becoming strict, we were clandestine in our movements, and we had security posted at every stop. I sensed that this group was becoming what I thought a good fighting unit should be. When I arrived in the platoon, Sergeant Hammonds and Sergeant Davey told on the very first night that things were loose. Some people were smoking pot. There were times when positions slept through the night. To be blunt, they had become careless, and they paid a terrible price for not being the strict force that they should have been.

Their lieutenant had been killed. Usually, the platoon sergeant is closer to the men than the officer. He sets the example and the expectations. It is the leadership of the platoon sergeant that determines how professional the fighting force will be. In this case, my platoon sergeant was failing miserably and by all accounts had done so for a long time, long before I arrived. I know there were trail watchers who observed each US fighting force that was in their area. The NVA observed which force to avoid and which group would be vulnerable. I knew this through all my stateside training. I knew this by trying to think like the enemy. We had to look and be professional at all times. "Never sacrifice security" were the words I took from my ranger training.

So…when I approached the two who were talking in a loud conversation, I told them to be quiet. The squad leader replied, "We're not cherries," the derogatory term given to the new soldiers in country, an obvious reference to me.

"Then act like it" was my short answer. They didn't like that I intended to bring some order to what had been going on. Again, they were such failures as soldiers, one being the platoon sergeant and the other a squad leader. I could only imagine the effect they had had upon the others. To this day, I wonder how they perceive their service time. "They will have to leave this unit, it is only a matter of time, and not soon enough."

And they did leave! They simply did not get on the helicopter one day as we took on a new mission. We are at times returned to base camp for overnight resupply, and then we CA out again for missions lasting one to five weeks. One day, they were not there. What happens so often was the "rear area" had a job opening because of soldiers leaving VN. When there is an opening and one has friends or when one has time in the field, you may be the one picked to return to the comfort and security of the rear.

Sergeant John Carlevero joined us as a squad leader in the resulting vacant spot. Sergeant Carlevero became very effective and was respected by the squad he led. Carlevero became our man who mastered making the mechanical ambushes, which protected our nighttime perimeters.

Back on Hill 1000, I have Labruna and others with me as we descend off the hill. I am carrying dozens of M-16 magazines with eighteen rounds in each, ready to hand off to the men below. We will exchange wounded and dead for the ammunition we are carrying. A young soldier is brought to us. We are able to put him on a litter carrier, and we begin our advance up the steep incline to a medevac chopper waiting to take him out. It is a difficult climb. The dirt is loose, and we slip, we slide, and yet progress is made. I'm thinking, *Got to get him to the top quickly!*

I see his right leg is attached to his body below the knee by skin and tissue. It dangles over the edge of the gurney. I don't know why, but I see very little blood. A medic must have stopped the bleeding. "Has he bled out?"

As we struggle up the steep incline, a jet streaks by strafing and then drops its ordinance. An explosion occurs, and bomb fragments strike the trees nearby. I'm almost oblivious to the noise, the sound of automatic machine gun fire, and the exploding bombs as other planes sweep through the valley. I turn at one time and think, "I can almost touch the wing of that jet." It's not real! The incline is so steep, the valley just wide enough for a jet to sweep through and strafe. The enemy is dug into the hillside below.

We make progress up the steep incline. It's hot and humid. I recall how tired I am, and I struggle to keep on my feet. At one point, the young soldier on the carrier cries out, "I'm going home. I'm going home." I encourage the carriers to move on, even though we are all worn. I think, *Going home, not for me. Can I survive this?* As we reach the top, a medevac chopper comes in. Its rotor blades are turning fast, giving off the sound of *wop-wop-wop.* We are clear of the landing zone, just at the edge of the hilltop waiting for the chopper to touchdown. As it descends slowly to the ground, it suddenly tips on its side. The rotor blades strike the ground. The blades continue turning, striking the ground, and the chopper advances toward us like slow motion. The blades stop turning less than twenty feet in front of us. The helicopter lies on its side. I have a straight-line frontal view of the pilot. He is slumped to the side that the chopper is leaning. The pilot took a round through his neck. Days later I try to analyze how this happened, as all the action was several hundred feet below the hill. A fifty-caliber machine gun must have been on an adjacent hilltop. A terrible lucky shot!

Men gather to render assistance to the pilot. I observe that when he is pulled from the fuselage, his head is dangling by tissue. Others push the disabled chopper over the side of the hill so that another chopper can land. We deposit the young man with the nearly severed leg onto the next helicopter. "Is this real?" I don't seem to make sense of the noise, the machine gun fire, and the exploding bombs below in the valley. "Is this going to happen every day? How do I survive this?"

We descend with more ammunition. We bring more dead and wounded to the top of Hill 1000. As we carry another wounded soldier of the 101st, he cries out, "I want to see my mother! I want to see my mother!" All day, the gunfire is intense. We climb the hill, clawing at footholds to bring the casualties to the top for the medevac. I think, *We have to keep moving. If I'm on this litter, I want the same effort from you guys!*

It was a blur. Days later we get the order to move quickly from the area. The ammo dump on Firebase Ripcord blew up when a Chinook helicopter bringing supplies was shot down landing upon the ammunition bunker. Total carnage! There is no more ammunition for the big guns to defend the base. Before that happened, each night we had retreated to our nighttime defensive position atop an adjacent hilltop. We watched the red tracer rounds going out from Firebase Ripcord and the green tracer rounds going in. These are spotter rounds every third round from the guns so that one can see the nighttime direction when firing: US forces used red, North Vietnamese used green. From our vantage point, it looked like the fireworks of a Fourth of July celebration. History tells us that after the ammo dump explosion, there were no means to continue the defense of Firebase Ripcord. History also records that there were nearly five thousand North Vietnamese regulars in the area compared to our single battalion of five hundred troops.

We were ordered to move out rapidly the next day. An arc light was scheduled to level the base and surrounding area. "Arc light" was the term used to describe B-52 bombers flying overhead at twenty-five thousand to thirty-five thousand feet and dropping one-thousand-pound bombs, saturating the area. We were to be at least one thousand meters away within hours so that the bombardment could begin. B-52s were already in route from Guam. We moved quickly and avoided walking the ridgeline trail, staying just below the ridge.

We continue to patrol the area assigned to the 101st Division. This area extends west to the Ashau Valley, which separates Laos from South Vietnam and south to the old provincial capital of Hue and north to the North Vietnamese border. It is the border that we must protect from the advancing North Vietnamese Army. The Ashau Valley is like a super highway following the Mekong River all the way to Saigon. The Ashau is the most heavily infiltrated area with advancing North Vietnamese regulars. It is our mission to stop this movement of men and supplies

Days later, our point man surprised the enemy in an outcropping of rocks. As the enemy flees in all directions, we drop to our stomachs and begin firing our weapons from our column position. Every other man fires left or right, raking the area with a barrage of lead. Upon ceasefire called, I notice the barrel of my M-16 is smoking hot. The toothbrush used for cleaning the weapon, stuck in the forward handgrip, has melted. We search the area, and the result, one enemy KIA and blood trails leading to an opening into a cave- like recess of rocks. Upon examination of the opening, I'm thinking it too dangerous and foolish to enter. I have in my possession several concussion grenades. These do not spread the lethal particles like the other grenades that we all carry. The concussion upon a person in a confined area is devastating. After lobbing one of these grenades, I stepped back to analyze the situation. Captain Newman with First Platoon joined us and called for powdered C-S gas to be delivered. The powder would be spread into the entrance of the cave to discourage further use.

Within a short time, we hear the helicopter overhead. The pilot was positioning his chopper so that he could make an airdrop of about twenty-five feet. The C-S powder was in a long rubber blivet approximately three to four feet long. It theoretically could withstand a drop of that height without breaking. The first blivet was pushed out the door and fell below. Unfortunately, the rubber, balloon-like container snagged on a tree branch. The snag caused the container to rip open. The downwash of the blades caused the powder to spread throughout our positions. We became blinded, and the C-S burned our nostrils. At the same time, I noticed the ground shaking around us, trees being blown into pieces, branches flying everywhere. All I heard was the sound of the helicopter.

I look around and think, *What's happening?* The pilot quickly abandoned his attempt to drop more C-S. He has confirmed that explosions were bursting around us. We were in the midst of a mortar attack! The helicopter had compromised our location. The C-S gas was smothering us. There was much havoc from the gas and from the attack as everyone tried to find cover.

PFC Gary Kiddy, machine gunner from Second Platoon and I both dived toward a depression in the ground. We kept our heads down as shrapnel, and ground particles pummeled our location. I felt someone tapping me on the shoulder. It was Captain Newman, our commander! He had determined, from the sound of the rounds leaving the mortar tube, the direction of the enemy firing upon our position. He pointed off to our left toward some high ground. Kiddy pointed his M-60 in the direction of the incoming mortar rounds while I fed the big gun the ammunition. After several minutes, firing several hundred rounds in the right direction, the mortar attack ceased. It was the captain's quick thinking that saved us that day! It was the M-60 machine gun firing in the right direction, which drove the enemy away to cover.

Kiddy took shrapnel into his right arm. My wristwatch was blown apart; I picked shrapnel from my right arm. Kiddy's wound was fairly significant. The medic looked at him and told the company commander that he should go in. A medevac chopper was called in. Kiddy walked to the chopper, and the medic jumped in with him! The medic saw his chance to get out of the field! Apparently he may have taken a little shrapnel also, as did most of us that day. We never saw him again. Kiddy survived. At ceremonies later, Kiddy received the bronze star w/v device for his actions. Several others were cited to receive purple hearts and awards for valor. Lieutenant Carpenter's M-16 took shrapnel that rendered it useless.

Lieutenant Carpenter had joined us days before. I welcomed him openly. I did not care for my position as platoon leader. Plus, I did not have a platoon sergeant in the position that I was comfortable with. After my platoon sergeant disappeared, headquarters sent out an E-6 staff sergeant. His MOS was a cook! I had trained stateside to be infantry! I went through some of the best training available at the time. As we lead patrols, the platoon leader is often number 2 in the line of file, behind the point man, advancing down the dense jungle trails. My position as platoon sergeant was to lead the platoon should our platoon leader become unable. I was in possession of maps, a compass for navigating, and I had my own radio operator. LT and I did not want to be physically close during movement; therefore, my position was near the rear of the column.

My ranger training told me movement single file on trails on ridgelines was dangerous even though the troops on the ground habitually moved in this fashion. Most often terrain dictates style of movement. A cunning enemy strategist can funnel you into a compromising death situation because of terrain.

LT, as I called him, was the second officer platoon leader within two months. I had been assigned to C Company, second platoon, at the end of in-country training. Lieutenant Sullivan, the previous platoon leader, had been killed days earlier while I was still in P training, along with several others in the ambush. I was immediately inserted into that position with the change of initial orders. I had intention of being assigned to L. Co., 75th Ranger Group. The ambush that killed Lieutenant Sullivan decimated Second Platoon. Until Lieutenant Carpenter arrived into the platoon, I served as the leader for several early missions and several following missions. Baptism by fire! I was thrust into a slot for a commissioned officer.

LT was a man determined to do well. He was smart. He talked rapidly, most always animated about some subject. He chain-smoked, was a lawyer by college education, and was trained in the military to supervise motor pool operations. Thus, initially he may have felt out of place in the world of the infantry soldier. I wish he had not told me that his MOS was motor pool officer. Nevertheless, I had great respect for this man who became my good friend. I trusted his decisions in the field. I liked that he included me in many of the decisions he had to make. What an awesome responsibility he had, knowing he had little experience in infantry tactics! Lieutenant Carpenter rose to each occasion that was brought upon him. But a toll was taken upon his emotional well-being at various times. On occasion, he left the bush for a short respite but always returned refreshed and ready to lead. LT and our company commander, Captain Newman, had deep mutual respect.

I received the operations order from LT. Today we go on a mission to retrieve bodies left on the field. A unit of the 327th was decimated during early morning extraction. The result was seven US soldiers killed and left behind. That was never to happen. Very unusual! We never leave our wounded or our dead upon the battlefield. I ask myself, "What kind of circumstances occurred that they left their KIA?"

During my stateside ranger training, as I was leading a patrol and being graded, we were "ambushed" by another group called the aggressors. The ranger responsible for grading my performance as a leader, pointed to one of my men and said, "You're dead." The ranger candidate fell to the ground and simulated being dead.

The instructor then looked at me and said, "Leave him, we have to move out quickly."

I replied, "No, I will carry him." With that I picked him up in a fireman's carry and proceeded to move out. It was a struggle as the ranger instructor noted my small stature and "killed" the biggest man in my patrol. I carried the KIA about 100 ft. when the instructor stopped me and said, "You passed your patrol, we never leave a fellow soldier behind on the battlefield.

C Company combat assaulted into the area with eight choppers. The door gunners open up with their M-60 machine guns before we are to land. Sitting on the edge of the helicopters with our legs dangling, the noise of the M-60 guns is deafening. The lead helicopters took fire from the ground below, the mission is called off, and our unit changes course. We CA into a different location and continue a search and destroy mission elsewhere. One week later, we return to the area to recover the KIAs. This time, there is no enemy return fire. When the helicopters land, we leap from both sides and remain in a prone position for a few long seconds to respond to enemy fire. There is none. My look falls upon a body just a few short yards away. It is now that I notice the stench of rotting flesh. I see the insects upon the body of the dead soldier.

The young man has no hair. It had fallen from his scalp onto the ground in a perfect pattern around the back of his head. I look away and try to blow the smell of death from my nostrils. Our mission is not to pick up and place the bodies into the body bag but to secure the area so that those with us could do this task. The smell of death was everywhere. As we fanned out in security positions we observed not seven bodies but nine killed in action left behind. After five to seven days lying in the hot humid sun, decomposition occurs quickly. I remember the outline of the body upon the soil as one man was rolled into the body bag. This was someone's son, perhaps a husband and maybe a father. The rubber bag was quickly zipped closed.

For many days and nights, I can't seem to get the image out of my mind, nor the smell of the rotting decaying bodies.

We talk about this event later. So demoralizing that these men were left behind! Such carnage, so much death! I piece together later from reports and try to analyze what happened. My conclusion, but not official: The unit of the 327th had been in a nighttime defensive position in that location the evening before. In the morning, they were to be extracted. The NVA had quietly moved within yards of their position during the night and were positioned in the morning to bring fire upon the Americans as they prepared to be extracted.

The helicopters were to land in a saddle between two small round hilltops. The hilltops were less than eight hundred feet apart with a low saddle between them, a perfect spot for an extraction. During the early morning hours of the extraction, the enemy was in position and opened up when the choppers came in, thus taking everyone by surprise. I'm adding that there apparently was little or no security or there had not been a quick sweep of the outside perimeter of the NDP before the extraction. From that day on, I was always conscious of proper security measures to be taken.

We returned to the area months later on another mission to search and destroy the enemy. We all knew this was the place! I still smelled death after dismounting from the chopper. I sensed that this was demoralizing among the men, to have to return to this nightmare! It certainly was to me!

3

We patrol for several days. We are extracted without incident. Our next mission takes us to a location where headquarters has determined enemy activity. It is late after we regroup from the insertion. This is a company-sized operation. We have three platoons with the company commander. Soon after insertion, Captain Newman talks with a nearby firebase to plot defensive targets. These are mapped predetermined locations, which give the nearby firebase immediate targets if we are attacked during the evening. Captain Newman asks for a marking round. These are white phosphorous artillery explosions in the air. I watch waiting for the explosion to occur overhead off to the south. There will be two predetermined targets recorded at the firebase. *Boom!* We see and hear the marking rounds. Great! Now we can settle in for the night with the knowledge that the FB 105 guns have us located and will be able to fire immediate support artillery if needed.

"Now what's happening?" Explosions begin occurring to the south within visual and getting closer to us. Captain Newman calls to the FB and yells, "Hold your fire, cease-fire, cease-fire!" The rounds are getting closer.

Firebase replies, "Those are not our rounds coming into your position."

It's getting dark; the enemy knows our location as they too observed the marking rounds that were called earlier or they saw us when we disembarked from the helicopters. We anticipate being attacked before daylight! They would much rather confront us in the darkness than in daylight. Word is passed quietly and quickly to grab onto the rucksack of the man in front of you. We begin walking in single file in the now nearly dark evening. Darkness comes early under the canopy. We move from this location to another, but it is treacherous as the jungle is thick and the terrain is rough. "Hang on tightly. Do not let go of the person in front or we will be separated." As we walked slowly, carefully in the darkness, word was passed down the line that the captain will lead us into a circle, and he will link up with the last person in the column. Thus we will have a perimeter established. What seemed like an hour, and the link is successful. We are now on 50 percent alert until daylight. We lie quietly on the jungle floor without digging in, waiting for light, anticipating the attack.

Morning light. No attack! If they were looking for us during the night, they did not determine our location. We are ordered to move out immediately to continue the search for the NVA. Now it is our turn again to be the hunter! We keep moving much of the morning. The captain is in charge of this operation. We stop near a clearing and a Red Cross medevac chopper comes for an extraction. As the bird sets down, the chopper becomes disabled and crashes to the ground. The pilot exits the downed chopper and immediately calls for another. I watch as the pilot removes the radio from the huey, and another comes in low for the extraction. Now we have a dilemma! A downed helicopter left for the enemy to salvage. Captain Newman orders me to remain behind with him as the entire company continues forward. Our order is to blow the chopper!

The captain hands the LAW (explosive rocket) to me and tells me to fire it into the fuselage, which will destroy the helicopter. I prepare for firing as there are two safety features that have to be removed before the LAW will fire. It misfires. Now we have to use a claymore mine to blow it with time-delay fuse. Together we rig the helicopter. We only have a few minutes as we know that time is important. We must join up with the rest of the company, but we cannot leave the helicopter without destroying it. I light the time-delay fuse, and we move out quickly. After a very short time, we hear the explosion. I think, *I just destroyed a half-million dollar helicopter!*

The two of us join up with the rest of the company. We proceed onward and find a likely defensible spot to spend the night. Sergeant Carlevero and others put out the mechanical claymores, which will defend the trails leading into our position. The claymores have trip wires set to go off if someone comes into our position. Intelligence forwards that there is much activity in the area. We prepare for a long night with 50 percent watch. We are close in a circle, the entire company of men. I can reach out on either side of my location and touch someone. We establish how and who will sleep and who will wake the next person. Again, we are on heightened alert as we are aware the enemy knows our location. It's just a matter knowing how they intend to attack. We are quite certain the attack will begin in the early hours.

One has to sleep. Without sleep, we are ineffective. Everyone knows what has to be done to keep himself rested but alert. Darkness turns to early morning light. Word is passed to prepare for a "mad minute" upon signal. During a mad minute, everyone fires on full automatic for one minute toward the outer perimeter. Just as we are about to open fire, one of the claymore mines has been tripped with a gigantic explosion. We hear voices shouting in Vietnamese. We begin our mad minute.

It is deafening, twenty-five to thirty soldiers loosening their ordinance in a sustained barrage. "Cease-fire!" Now it is quiet beyond the perimeter. How many were out there? The foliage is so dense one cannot see beyond three meters. LT and I gather up four others, and on command, we walk toward the killing zone continuously firing our weapons. What is beyond? There is more shouting in Vietnamese as we advance into a clearing. It is here that we see the carnage. We notice human blood and body parts from the effect of the mechanical ambush. There is one enemy who was left behind. The claymore took both legs from the knees down. He must have been the first one on the trail. I look upon the soldier with sorrow. "Did he have a family? Who was this young man?" We search the body for papers finding none. For some reason, I am pleased we found nothing. After reporting back to the captain, we continue our movement through the densely forested jungle.

Every day is different, every day is monotonous, same old same old. We rise in the morning from our holes and positions, we urinate. We cautiously look and listen for enemy movement nearby. We heat our coffee in a tin cup by burning high explosive C-4. Remarkably an eight-ounce cup will boil in six to seven seconds. As Sergeant Hammonds told me earlier, "You like sugar and creamer, don't deny yourself, this is Vietnam." You change your socks every day, as you don't want to sleep with wet socks in your boots. Your boots are on; never sleep without them.

A dry pair of socks keeps you mobile and pain-free. When you change your socks, we place the wet pair on our chest. By morning, this pair is dry. We change to the dry pair. After several days with wet socks, the skin on your feet rubs off with little friction. This is the most painful part of negligence. Medic Doc Soltero makes his rounds several times per week to look at the feet of our platoon. He reports to me. Sometimes a soldier neglects his feet or neglects taking the malaria pill.

Today, Soltero says I must talk to Poncho. Oscar is our grenadier carrying an M-203 launcher. His feet are bad. He neglected to change socks regularly. Within a short time with temperature and moisture conditions changing, your feet become subjected to jungle rot, including immersion foot.

I seek out Oscar. I love this guy! Oscar never complains. Oscar carries a heavy load in comparison to his size. He has the most pleasant smile always; he has a sister who writes encouraging letters to me. I love this man to no end. I find Oscar on the perimeter, and I say, "Oscar, let me see your feet."

"No, Sarge, I'm fine," he says.

"Take the boots off," I order. After removing his boots, I wince. His feet are devoid of 15–20 percent of skin tissue. "Oscar, you can't stay out here. You have to go in. You can't walk like this."

"No, Sarge, I don't want to go in." I ask why not, and he replies that his friends are here. My heart melts. Oscar prefers to stay with friends in the jungle, subjecting himself to possible death, to the discomfort of sleeping on the wet jungle floor, exposing himself to the leaches and fire ants that crawl all over his body, subjecting himself to the mosquitoes, jungle rot, cold evenings on the ground, no hot meals—always C-rations. Infantry always infantry! I love you, man! Oscar has to go in to heal.

Years later, I try to locate Oscar from the phone book out of Avila, Texas. I am calling from North Dakota. I ask the operator to help me locate this man. "I don't know his number, but he is from Avila, Texas."

She says she will try to assist, but once she looks at the directory from Avila, she responds, "There are over twenty Oscar Gonzaleses listed." I still want to find Oscar!

Another time, George Swantek became ill. Doc Soltero says he has a fever. He had been feverish all day; now it is just before dark, and he is in a four-man position. We are getting ready to set up our perimeter guard. Each position determines how they want to be on guard. Doc asks me to take a look. I approach Swantek's position. He is lying on his side, on the ground, and his whole body is shaking, shivering. Obviously he's very cold. His back is to me. I lean down, and I ask, "How are you doing, George?"

He answers in his New York accent, "I'm freezing. I'm cold." I tell the others in the position that he can't pull guard tonight. They are to make arrangements to deal with it. Also, I'll be there with him throughout the night.

We won't call for an extraction. Requesting a medevac chopper to come at night is dangerous for the crew, and it compromises our position. The enemy notes our location. The medevac pilots are outstanding. If you called them, they would come under any circumstance. These were the unsung heroes of the time. Countless lives were saved because of their absolute disregard for personal safety. It's out of the question. George is not leaving nor would he want to sacrifice the platoon's safety. George is moaning, audibly. *I don't know. Is it malaria?* This happens even if you take the required pills each Friday every week. George is an outstanding soldier. He will walk point anytime he is asked to do so. Larry Thostenson and George were often in point position! The point man can be blown away first in an encounter on the trail.

To be in point man position, one has to have the ability to not just look but to see all the signs—signs which would indicate something amiss. One needs a sixth sense to recognize danger. This is the most important position during movement. The fate of the unit lies in the hands of the point man.

My ranger training comes to mind. "George, I am going to lie behind you. I am going to wrap my arms and legs around you, and you will feel the heat of my body."

"Okay," he says. "But don't try doing anything," an obvious reference.

I pulled a poncho over us, and within minutes, George settles down, his body quits shaking. He was wet from fever, wet from the hard trek through the jungle. The cool night air and damp ground made him miserable. Years later, George remembered the incident and growled, "I didn't know what you were up to, but it worked." George did not go in that next day.

My constant fear was that my mistake would cause a loss of life. Each day so many intricacies are in an operation. Such was the time we had to be resupplied because of lack of water and supplies. Our CO had determined a supply point on a ridgeline.

We had been low on water for several days. In the hot humid air, it doesn't take long for a soldier to become ineffective because lack of water. When you lose the ability to sweat, you are already in trouble from the heat. We had been down into the low valley but found no streams flowing. The decision was to go back up on top the ridgeline and get supplied by chopper, providing we could find a landing zone.

The trees were very tall, sometimes seventy-five to one hundred feet. The helicopters needed a clearance line from two sides if it was to land. It was getting dark. We need to be in a position that is defendable, meaning on higher ground than the enemy. We needed that high ground above to spend the night.

The captain determined it was too late to move any farther. We were clinging to the hillside when the order came down that this was it! Going no farther up. The incline was steep, maybe like an 8/12 pitch on a roofline. It was difficult to stand, and this is where we are staying for the night!

Everyone is quiet. We know the risks of leaving higher ground above us. The enemy could easily rake our position from above if they knew our location. I heard not a sound as the men prepared to manage the watch with whomever they were lying beside.

It was near total darkness. Suddenly a string of profane words came from one position. It was S/Sgt. Hughes. We all recognized his gravelly voice. Absolutely no one could swear like Staff Sergeant Warren Allen Hughes! Sarge was the oldest soldier in the company. He was on second tour. He was a good infantry soldier, but he had a drinking problem and always got into trouble back in the base camps. He functioned best in the field. His position was First Platoon, platoon sergeant. We were in a company operation again. Then it was quiet. I could not help but wonder what set this man off in a setting like we were in. Very unusual! S/Sgt. Hughes (Staff Sergeant) never drank in the field, so I knew this was not the problem.

Morning came, and we found out what set S/Sgt. Hughes off so profanely. A monkey had come down from a tree and stole the canteen he had laid aside. It was the last of his water!

The captain sent a squad from Second Platoon, led by Sergeant Davey, to secure the LZ (landing zone) spotted the day before. When the squad approached the potential LZ, they were attacked by small arms fired and rocket-propelled grenades (RPG). Sergeant Davey reacted by returning fire and brought the squad back to reconnoiter and to report. We needed that LZ to be secure for extraction and for resupply.

Captain Newman ordered LT to take two to three men to climb the hill around the left side of the LZ. I was to take two to three men around the right side. After climbing up and over the ridgeline, I was in position. We were below the LZ, advancing parallel to the north just forty feet or so from the top of the ridgeline. Our weapons will be on full firepower, fully automatic as we advance around the perimeter on each side approaching each bunker. We are to link up on the far north end, thus securing ground on both sides of the landing zone. After LT and I secure the perimeter, the remaining unit will advance across the top approaching from the south of the LZ.

We begin the assault. My M-16 can fire an eighteen round clip in three to four seconds. I know the need to be careful in using the ammunition. I began firing the moment I hear the gunfire from LT's group on the left. We move rapidly, approaching each bunker, weapons firing in short bursts of three to four rounds. I rake the first bunker and move to the second. I stick the muzzle of my 16 into the next bunker and pull the trigger. Nothing happens! The new full magazine had dropped from the weapon before it clicked secure in place. Fortunately, there was no return fire in this bunker. I used to have nightmares of this incident. We continue onward around the sides of the LZ. I spot LT on the north end to my left, according to the plan. The remaining unit comes across the top advancing northward. Just as they reach the far north edge and off to my left, there is a tremendous explosion. An artillery round had been hidden in a tree and was command detonated. Several wounded, one KIA. Our medic, new to the unit for this operation, died with shrapnel to the skull. His helmet was not on his head but tied in back to his rucksack.

I knew I had failed in that moment. I should have moved further to the north after LT and I linked up. Had we advanced another twenty yards down the trail we would have flushed those waiting to blow the artillery. Choppers were called in to extract the KIA and wounded. We waited to be supplied. I walked over the hillside and let my tears flow; my gut began retching! I felt responsible. I was responsible! I could have prevented this tragedy. He was new in country.

Another moment, another mission as we combat assault more than twenty-five different times into different areas of operation. Sometimes we are sent to the lowlands to relieve another force that went in for a stand-down. Stand-downs are periods of time when an infantry unit goes back to a secure area for a short time for in-country relaxation.

It's near monsoon season. We have orders to set up two nighttime ambushes in the vicinity of a wide riverbed. Third platoon will set up clandestinely on a small island in the middle of the river. The company commander will remain with First Platoon in a defensive position on high ground downriver from the sandbar island. The island has dense short trees and bamboo growing. The riverbed is about two hundred feet across. The flowing water is shallow, and Third Platoon can walk to the island and prepare for the nighttime ambush. They will set out directional claymores on both sides of the island to interdict the foot traffic expected that evening. Traveling by river in the shallow water is much easier than cutting your way through the underbrush on the riverbanks. This is a frequent avenue of movement by the NVA.

Captain Newman ordered me to take Second Platoon to set up an ambush on the high ground adjacent to the men down on the riverbed. We are about twenty feet above the flowing riverbed and several hundred yards from the other positions. We set up our positions and put out our mechanical devices and wait. It is total darkness, no stars overhead. The skies are overcast, and it is apparent we will get wet. It begins to rain! The drops of water are like nothing I had ever seen before. The skies just opened up, the lightning and thunder was beyond belief! It was during the lightning strikes that we could see somewhat in front of us; otherwise, total blackness. My wet glasses hindered my vision. They fogged up. How am I ever going to see someone passing in front of me?

My RTO is monitoring the radio. We begin to hear the Third Platoon chatter calling back to the company commander indicating the water is rising rapidly. Captain Newman orders the men to return to the high ground. Minutes pass, and another transmission from Third Platoon, "The water is flowing so fast we can't make it to the riverbank." The captain says to leave all ordinance and quickly move out. Another transmission, "We are stranded. We are hanging onto the shrubs and trees trying to stay above water."

Captain Newman radioed my location and said he was coming through our ambush site. Make sure all mechanicals are controlled so that we do not kill our own. Within minutes, I meet the captain on the trail. One other soldier, PFC Gary Kiddy, follows him. Kiddy volunteered to help with the rescue, as he was a strong swimmer. They are carrying a rope. Newman's plan is to swim out to the island and attach the rope so others can come to the riverbank safely. He also called for helicopters to retrieve the men off the island. I wondered how the pilot could find us in this downpour? Within minutes, I hear the chopper overhead in the distance.

After what seemed like an hour, the rescued members of Third Platoon came through our ambush site. I am told that we lost one soldier being swept away. Captain Newman was swept away also, but he was tethered by the rope and pulled to safety. He took on a lot of water, so he was placed on a chopper and taken back to base camp, barely conscious. The captain remained in the hospital for several days. By morning, the rain stopped. We went back down to the riverbed to pick up what we could find of the ordinance left behind. We did not find PFC Harvel until midmorning several hundred yards downriver. His body was snagged on debris left by the fast-moving waters. On his person, he had all his ammo, too much weight to make it to safety.

Much later, Captain Newman is awarded the Soldier's Medal for his actions during this operation in rescuing the men under his command, having done so with complete disregard for his personal safety.

We continue on with our forward observer serving as company commander in Captain Newman's absence. Several days go by, and we reach an area that would make a beautiful resort retreat. Here we see sparkling pools of water. The river has carved out a circular winding path that is screaming for all of us to jump in and clean our bodies. The sun is shining brightly. What an opportunity to cleanse ourselves! The platoon leaders and the acting company commander, Terry Morrison, think it safe and a good idea to let the men enjoy the water, but we must put out security first! We post security on the high ground all around. After noting security is in place, we are allowed to cleanse ourselves. I'll never forget the smiles as the men played in the water. Within a short time, a helicopter flies overhead, very low, and it lands. Out steps the battalion commander wanting to know what's going on, and he does not appear to be happy with what he sees. I am not in on any conversation, but I think First Lieutenant Terry Morrison got reprimanded, even though we had security posted all around. It was a good moment for the troops!

Periodically we received supplies at a drop-off point in the jungle from the helicopters. The choppers are our lifelines. We receive our C-rations, clean clothing, water, additional ammo, mail, and a box every two or three weeks or so-called SPs. This box is about 18" × 18" × 18". It contains the following but not limited to writing paper, candy but no chocolate, a dozen packs of four cigarettes and four cigarillos, mail from the USO, which encouraged civilians to write to us, paperbacks (ironically I read *Love Story* in the jungle, "Loving someone means never having to say I'm sorry"), and cool aid tablets to make the water in our canteens more palatable! This container was to supply a platoon of fifteen men. It was heavy and awkward to carry. It usually took two men to move it to the location where it was intended to be after a drop by the helicopter.

Our daily food, in four-to-six-ounce cans, consisted of the following basic meals called C-rations, which one consumed when you were able or whenever you were hungry: lima beans, scrambled eggs, chili con carne, crackers, cheese, deserts like pound cake, canned fruit (peaches), fruitcake, and a small roll of toilet paper. If someone had to be extracted for nonlife threatening reasons, it was rumored that Steve Nyguard always negotiated laying claim upon the pound cake before that soldier left the field!

Speaking of Nyguard, we were on the trail moving somewhat sporadically because of a time frame that allowed us to move slowly. I was in position of platoon sergeant, which meant I was in the rear of the column with my RTO and two rear security soldiers behind me. Their responsibility was to be aware of anyone approaching us from our rear side as we moved forward. Their position was extremely important as trail watchers could easily attack from the rear. We were halted in our movement for a time, which seemed uncomfortable to me. LT indicated we were to rest in place. I sent Nyguard just off the trail back about twenty feet to a higher elevation so he could observe if anyone was following us. We sat in place for about twenty minutes, and then the order came down that we were moving out.

We proceeded without Steve. My mistake! I assumed that the soldier next in line with Steve would alert him to our moving. Didn't happen! We stopped again after several hundred yards. From the rear, suddenly Steve appeared coming up the trail, quite agitated and sweating from his movement to catch us. He got right into my space and quite firmly reminded me that we had left him behind, alone in the jungle! That was all that was said about that incident. It could have been a disaster for Steve! These are the intricacies of each day!

As a platoon sergeant, I always made contact with each night-time position after every stop for the evening. I would spend a little time with each position, talking with the men about different things, getting to know them, listening to their concerns, sharing personal comments, plus making sure they had their guard rotation set up for the evening. One late afternoon, we moved into position just before darkness. I scrambled to ready my position and then moved around the perimeter on the inside approaching each position quietly but not to startle the men. I came to a position manned by Reyes, Culp, and Gonzales.

I saw that all three were in a prone position and no-one-on guard facing outward. I whispered loud enough for them to hear had they been awake. This was early. Apparently they wanted to catch a quick shut-eye before rotation, or the first guard decided to chance a quick restful moment by closing his eyes. I recognized Culp facing inward, his weapon lying on the ground pointing inward instead of outward. Again I made an audible noise, which startled Culp from his sleep. He immediately scrambled to his knees and grabbed his weapon, which was pointing in my direction. The weapon discharged. I felt the powder from the round burn my left cheek. One round fired in the night, directly but luckily missing me. Several things occurred at this incident: his weapon was pointed in, he had fallen asleep, the weapon was not on safe, and he came close to killing his platoon sergeant! He was careless and had succumbed to fatigue without thinking security first. If we were to explore the number of casualties caused by accidents during this war, we would find a number larger than what is acceptable. Fatigue is always a factor.

We always knew our deros date. That was the date that our Vietnam tour was complete. I would hear troops say, "Twenty-eight days and a wake-up." Twenty-nine days, and this soldier was on his way back to "the world"! Everyone kept track of the time left. The tour was to be 365 days, but most everyone was able to go home early. Most often going home early was thirty days or less. As one got closer to his deros date, one became acutely aware of the possibility of not reaching that goal. What could go wrong may go wrong!

There were stories about death in the last days of the tour.

LT went back to base camp for personal reasons, and we continued onward with more missions. It was the beginning of the monsoon season, which could last three months. It would rain with little warning, clouds coming over above so quickly. We CA'd out from base camp at Phu Bae. It was a company-sized operation. I was acting platoon leader in LT's absence. Captain Newman reassigned S/Sgt. Hughes from Third Platoon to my platoon to act as my platoon sergeant. The captain had two motives for assigning Hughes to my platoon. First, I needed a platoon sergeant since I moved up, but secondly, the captain was punishing Hughes for his behavior back at base camp. S/Sgt. Hughes was in trouble with the captain because of the night before. Hughes, in a drunken moment, caused a fight with individuals from another company. When he learned that he was to be under my leadership, it was supposed to be humiliating to him, exactly what the captain wanted. However, to this day, I doubt Hughes was humiliated. We had been friends from the beginning.

Understand this, I had great respect for S/Sgt. Hughes. I felt that he had similar thoughts toward me. We had many conversations together, many very personal conversations. He came into country when I did, but he was assigned to Third Platoon. S/Sgt. Hughes had the same rank as I, but he had time in the service, twelve years compared to my service time of eighteen months, which militarily allowed him to outrank me.

When we boarded the choppers to CA out, I was on first chopper, and Hughes was to follow on the second chopper. My group of six lifted off. The pilot dropped us off into the jungle, and lo and behold, the others were not behind in the landing. We had exited the helicopter, moved to the tree line, regrouped, and waited. "They're not coming!" I found out days later that Hughes had a liquor bottle in his hand when he attempted to board, and the door gunner told him to throw it away, which he did. Unfortunately, the bottle struck a rotating rotor blade. The pilot immediately shut the chopper down.

Here we are! Six of us, and the rest of the company nowhere in sight, and we have no knowledge of where they are. "Are they still at base or are they dropped off in a different location?" My RTO, Barney Bad-Ass, has the call sign and frequency. He contacts the company commander, and he informs me they were dropped in a different location. He gives me his map coordinates using the SOI security codes. After plotting my location, I determine the rest of the company is five to six kilometers away, fortunately on the same ridgeline. We should join up in three to four hours. Got to get there before dark!

Reyes volunteers to walk point. Reyes is a good-looking Hispanic with a nice smile. Movement is slow. I follow Reyes about fifteen yards back. This is the first that Reyes has been point. He is good, he is cautious. Not only does he have to be cognizant of trip wires, depressions in the ground where a compression explosive may be buried and try to foresee those lying in wait on the sides, he has to listen and observe intently to his immediate surroundings. I want him to go slowly, but it is getting late! When Lieutenant Sullivan was killed on the trail, the point man was allowed through the "kill zone" before they blew the ambush. Typical! The point man is usually several yards out front from the rest of the column. Let him pass, then blow the explosives when the column tightens up. Understand, the military is like an athletic team in a sense. We discuss after action reports when time allows. We talk about what happened and what to do in the future. I know the day Lieutenant Sullivan was killed, he was ordered to move rapidly so they could reach a destination for extraction. Sergeant Hammonds told me this story soon after I joined the group. I was aware of the incident this day as we moved to join the company. We linked up late that day.

The next morning, the captain issues his operation order. Second platoon will descend to the valley to a flowing river. We are instructed to walk the shallow riverbed toward an upstream destination. We are to join up with the remaining company approximately 1,500 kilometers away as they move to another location for the night. I repeat the instructions to the CO, "We are to walk the riverbed?"

"Correct" was the reply. We descend down to the valley and begin our trek up river. I can't help but see the high ground on three sides of us. "This is insane." We are in a kill zone for anyone on either side of the riverbank. I stop the column and motion everyone to move to the right near the bank. I call to S/Sgt. Hughes to come forward. He looks worried. I see it in his face, and I know that he is thinking the same as I. We make the decision to climb the riverbank and proceed on the same azimuth cutting our way through the "wait a minute vines" and brush. The going is extremely slow. The point man uses his machete to cut a trail.

Soon it is apparent that we will not link up before dark. I radio the company commander to inform him of our progress. I'm prepared for the anger in his voice but not expecting the way he said it. My call sign being 1-9, he informs me the quickest way to reach our destination in a triangular setting is to travel the hypotenuse. The CO had been a math teacher! Traveling above the riverbank put us on two legs of the triangle. Furthermore, "One-nine, you were to draw fire upon yourselves!"

We are now on the riverbank and have to find a somewhat defensible nighttime position. The ground is flat but covered with heavy foliage. We set up our circular perimeter. I take the position on the trail that we just cut, with two others, Barney, my RTO, and Sergeant Charlie Graff, who just recently joined us. It begins to rain, and it rains buckets, very hard! The lightning is intense. We took time to tie a poncho to small sturdy shrubs to keep the water off our heads. We need to be able to see somewhat, plus we have learned you take all measures to avoid these huge raindrops. After a quick visual of our tight perimeter, I slip back under the poncho and take third watch that will ensure that I'm on last watch the second time around. I watch from 11:00 p.m. to 1:00 a.m., then 4:00 a.m. to first light.

Shortly after my first watch, I am awakened with a start. The NVA are coming up the trail! They have flashlights, and they are singing, just slightly audible but definitely a tune! I grab my weapon and focus on Charlie Graff sitting in front of me. Charlie is on guard, but he isn't concerned! It is then that I see his right hand is raised holding onto the edge of the poncho, and there is a song coming from his mouth! I see his left arm pushing up in the middle of the poncho, his right arm pulling downward at the same time. As he does so, a gush of water flows over the side. The lightning is all around us. During each flash, I'm able to see what Charlie is doing. He's keeping the water from collapsing the tent while humming a tune. It was a bad dream but much better than it being real! My heart is pounding. I'm still shaking sleep and trying to get my mind clear. "Charlie, what are you doing?" I ask. He just smiles at me. Charlie's way of finding courage through the night, or is this his way of staying awake?

I first met Charlie Graff after being in country for about two weeks. Our company came in out of the field for an overnight stand-down for resupply. After preparing our rucks for the next day, three of us walked the two blocks to the enlisted men's club. We sat and ordered a beer. We were seated for about five minutes when another soldier came over and started talking to Davy. I did not pay a lot of attention on what was said among the two, but it was apparent that they knew each other well. Sergeant Davy related to the soldier about where we had been operating, how things were going, etc. He then introduced me as the current platoon sergeant for Second Platoon. That is when Charlie left rather hurriedly.

Davy then proceeded to tell me about Charlie Graff. Charlie came in to the country as an E-5. He had attended the same NCO school that I had attended. Sergeant Graff then shipped over to Vietnam and spent just a short time in the field when he decided he did not want to go back out. He then did the paperwork declaring that he was a conscientious objector opposed to the war. He could not "in good conscience carry a weapon." Charlie remained in the rear secure area awaiting the outcome of his request. It was quite obvious to all in the unit that Charlie was headed toward a confrontation with the US military. Conscientious objector status is usually determined before entering the military. In other words, he had a most unlikely chance of succeeding in his request. The result would be stockade time and a dishonorable discharge, which would be on his record for a lifetime. Charlie was basically lying low in the rear area trying to avoid a confrontation with superiors.

When Captain Newman joined the company as commander, he reviewed the names of the men assigned to his company. That is when he noted Sergeant Graff's status. He arranged a meeting with Graff and convinced him to come back out to the field. He would not have to carry a weapon. He would become the company commander's RTO. Thus he was assigned to go back into Second Platoon until he would link up with Captain Newman. The night that Charlie Graff set up with me as described, he was without a weapon.

We reached the command post location by noon the next day. I had sent a message to the CO that we were within distance, and they were ready to receive us through their perimeter. Nothing more was said to me by the captain. To this day, I wonder whether he thought I made good judgment. It was simple to see how easy it would be for a machine gun to rake the riverbed, literally annihilating Second Platoon within seconds. In military jargon, one calls this a "command decision on the ground." S/Sgt. Hughes remained with me for several more days until LT Carpenter joined us again. I had great respect for this grizzled "old man." "He knew his stuff" as we would say when you recognized a good soldier performing his duty.

I always set up with the new recruits on their first night into the platoon. It would always be my RTO, the new recruit, me, and sometimes one other person in a position. The number depended upon our strength in the field and how the terrain dictated our defense. Sometimes in a platoon-sized mission, we could defend a perimeter with four positions; sometimes it would take five positions. You always got more sleep with four people in a position, and we needed our rest as we moved constantly throughout the day. Our rucksacks weighed anywhere from sixty to eighty pounds on our backs. It was a load, especially in the hot humid air. You wonder, how could one position into fighting maneuvers with so much weight on our backs? We would drop our rucks, if needed, and then proceed without them. In addition, we also had pistol belts that stayed with us with containers for ammo magazines and hand grenades.

That first night for a tall, skinny blond soldier was his worst night of his young life. I set up with Stretch. He was quiet and very afraid. My heart went out to guys like this. By this time, I had seen men react in so many different ways during their various experiences. Tonight Stretch was unable to calm his fears. He was scheduled to take second watch the first time around. I would take last watch. Others would fill in the watch between the two of us. I sat with stretch during his watch in the two-man fighting position, dug wide, and deep. One other to be in the guard rotation lay on the ground behind us. I should have been sleeping preparing for my first watch rotation. Stretch was crying softly sitting next to me. I did not want to leave the hole and lie prone on the ground until I thought he was able to do his first watch.

He was so distraught he wasn't thinking rationally. I kept whispering, "It'll be all right. Don't worry so much. Think of positive things." Near the end of his watch, he quieted, and I was able to determine that he was sleeping. He was exhausted from fear! I let him sleep through the rest of his watch, taking it for him. When my watch was completed, I stayed in the hole with Stretch to do his time. Sometimes men in combat are reduced to being boys, then have to fight back to become a man again! Eventually Stretch became a reliable good soldier in the platoon.

When the rainy monsoon season first started, we welcomed the change from the hot humid air that seemed to stick on us in every location on our bodies. We wore jungle fatigues that allowed the dampness to readily leave the material like our modern-day athletic gear. We did not wear underclothing, as that would impede the drying. Those who opted to wear the boxer shorts in the jungle soon discovered the wet clothing began chafing on their butts and thighs, causing the skin to peel off. The jungle was very damp under the canopy of the towering trees. It never seemed to dry out. At times the foliage was so thick we had to use machetes to cut our way through. Within this dampness lived many creatures that loved to infest our bodies. Leaches, fire ants, and mosquitoes were everywhere, hoping to attach to our skin.

I was most cautious about the leaches. I saw what a leach could do. At times there were dogs assigned to walk with the point man as they were trained to sniff out the enemy. The dogs did not last long in the jungle. The leaches would enter the orifices of the dog (penis, butt, ears, etc.). We tied a strap around our legs just below the knee to keep leaches from crawling any higher. If a leach got under your clothing, you sometimes did not know it until you did a body check, or sometimes, it gorged itself on your blood so much that when it was bumped or pressed, it split open, leaving a bloody area on your clothing. They were difficult to pull off when they were attached for a few hours. We carried a very strong repellant that made them drop immediately. The repellant was for the mosquitoes also.

One of the first things we did after awakening in the morning was to check for leaches. You simply dropped your pants and ran your hands up and down your inner thighs, around your butt and privates, hoping not to find one of these bloodsucking creatures. We were in a company operation, and one morning, I witnessed a soldier having the medic remove a leach from his eyeball. The medic put a drop of repellant on the end of the leach, and it dropped immediately. The damage was done however; the soldier's eyeball was bright red like a small tomato. He was sent back to the rear. I never saw him again but heard that he lost his sight in that one eye. There were times when we sat on the trail lying back on our rucksacks that I played this little game. How many leaches will crawl toward me within the five to ten minutes that we are stopped? Leaches sense the body heat, and they are constantly hungry for your blood! When I returned from Vietnam, it took fully two to three years for the leach scars to fade from my lower legs.

Then the monsoon season brought more discomfort. Now we were constantly wet and cold. Imagine as wet as one would be if you fell into a lake with your clothing on. That was monsoon season all day and for weeks at a time. At night, there would be some respite, as we would cover our bodies with ponchos that were waterproof or share a small tent that we could gather under during our night defensive positions. It was then that we made sure an extra pair of socks was on our chest to be dry by morning. We were cold at fifty degrees and wet through and through. These conditions brought on the immersion skin conditions.

Because of the monsoon weather, we stayed in our night defensive positions longer than usual each morning before moving out to another location in search of the enemy. It was during this time that the imaginative gourmet cooks in the platoon put their concocted C-rations together and made a dish for others to sample. It was also time to write letters and to resume reading from the books that most carried in their rucksacks.

We never stayed more than one night in the same location, always moving to another NDP site each day. We had to make progress on the map as our location was recorded back at TOC headquarters. Somewhere in the room was a huge map, and every unit was plotted. We knew that if you did not move, headquarters became very upset and ordered us to change positions. Sometimes that meant giving up a high defendable position to a less defendable one just for the sake of movement or standard operating procedures (SOP).

Such was the case when First Platoon elected to stay a second night in their NDP. Each evening, we had to radio back to HQs relaying our location. Thus it became known that First Platoon did not move. The battalion commander ordered the platoon to move even as the darkness had enveloped the area. Members of the platoon tried to retrieve their protective claymores positioned around their perimeter. The terrain was steep, and in the darkness, one soldier fell into a precipice and was injured. The platoon sergeant who was acting platoon leader radioed back to HQ that it was too dark, too dangerous to move, and they were staying another night. He determined the next defendable position too far away.

The colonel back at HQ ordered the platoon sergeant to move the platoon. The sergeant responded by saying, "Negative, sir." HQ relieved him of command on the spot, telling him that the First Squad Leader is now in charge. Again, the battalion commander ordered First Squad Leader to move. And once again, the squad leader responded, "Negative, sir." The angry battalion commander informed the sergeants that they would be picked up by helicopter in the morning to answer to the charge of disobeying a direct order. I didn't know the outcome of the pending judgment. Later I had a face-to-face talk with the injured soldier, and his injuries from the fall were still visible.

Captain Newman, Company Commander, C Company, retired as a colonel from the US Army. Captain Newman was awarded the Soldier's Medal for heroic action not involving a hostile force. He was also awarded our nation's third highest honor with the Silver Star Medal because of his actions against a hostile force. Both awards were well deserved.

The author, S/Sgt William Henderson in 1971
just prior to leaving Vietnam.

In Loving Memory of

Robert Gallardo Soltero

August 23, 1950 – September 22, 2004

Robert "Doc" Soltero, 2nd Platoon medic received the Silver Star Medal for heroic action during his tour in Vietnam. Robert was in much demand by the battalion as he was considered the best of medics.

Steve Nyguard from Maple Grove, MN, and the author S/Sgt William Henderson from North Dakota.

101st Airborne Div. troopers jump from a hovering helicopter as   Vietnam. Bad terrain prevented the chopper from landing. T
...set out on a mission 20 miles southwest of Hue in northern South   troopers are with C Co. of the division's 2nd Bn., 501st Inf   (US.

A scene showing the rough landing zone (LZ) where soldiers of C Company were required to dismount by leaping from the hovering helicopter. Sixty to eighty pound rucksacks made for a hard landing.

S/Sgt Henderson and platoon member, Sgt George Swantek from New York on the day they were to leave Vietnam.

Eight members of 2nd Platoon posing on a firebase near the demilitarized zone in northern South Vietnam.

Left to right: S/Sgt Henderson, George Swantek, Charlie Graf, Steve Nyguard, David (Punky) Stevenson, Robert (Doc) Soltero, LT Mike Carpenter from Maine and Ralph Labruna from New Jersey. I have the highest respect for this group of fine soldiers.

Second platoon being inserted on a rough LZ. Two combat soldiers sat on each side of the chopper while two more sat in the middle behind the pilots. Our feet dangled over the edge but we were unable to touch the skids. This made for easy and quick dismount. Total capacity was ten military personnel with the two pilots and two door gunners.

Bring in the birds for an insertion, a US Army photo, April 12, 1971.

Stretch Walker, William Pinkstock, Doc Soltero from Tucson, AZ, Larry Thostenson from Minnesota and Barney (Bad-ass) Congdon from South Dakota.

Steve Nyguard from Maple Grove, Mn and George Swantek from New York.

The 101st Airborne patch with the author's ranger tab across the top. The rifle above the patch signifies the wearer earned the CIB which is the combat infantry badge.

Eight members of 2nd platoon. Kneeling left to right Oscar Gonzales from La Vila, Texas and LT Carpenter, platoon leader. Standing, "Punky" Stevenson from Mt View, Missouri, Sgt John Carlevero from Texas, George Swantek from New York, Steve Nyguard from MN, A Vietnamese soldier, Barney Congdon, the platoon RTO, and Ralph Labruna from New Jersey.

Larry Thostenson from Maple Grove, MN and "Doc" Soltero, Tucson, AZ. Larry had a habit of saying "Oh Man" if he did not like the situation at hand. Larry was one of many who walked point when called upon. Doc was the most respected medic in the battalion. Both soldiers were exceptional at their assignments.

David Stevenson, Steve Nyguard, Ralph Labruna and George Swantek were not only good at what they were assigned to do but were exceptional individuals as friends in the platoon.

Captain Newman, C company commander and Orlando Bacca from New Mexico.

An in-country R&R at Eagle Beach along the coast of South Vietnam. S/Sgt Bill Henderson, LT Carpenter and Steve Nyguard.

The first reunion of 2nd platoon veterans in Minneapolis area in 1983. Back row Gayland (Davey) Davis, Doug Ryder, George Swantek, Steve Nyguard, Front row Doc Soltero, Larry Thostenson, Bill Henderson, Mike Carpenter and Ralph Labruna.

Sgt Gayland Davis (Davey), LT Mike Carpenter, Ranger Bill Henderson, and Barney (Bad-ass) Congdon the platoon RTO. Taken atop Coc-a-Bo Mountain near the DMZ in northern South Vietnam. LT Carpenter went on as a civilian to become the Attorney General for the state of Maine.

George Swantek, Steve Nyguard and Ralph Labruna. Absolutely the finest soldiers that I had the privilege to serve with while touring the Republic of South Vietnam.

PLACE: THUA THIEN PROVINCE

         REPUBLIC OF SOUTH VIETNAM

TIME: 1970-1971

MISSION: JUST STAY ALIVE

Our mission during this time in our lives was to "Just Stay Alive."

S/Sgt Warren Allen Hughes, one of the finest soldiers in the bush. The "Old Goat". S/Sgt Hughes was the oldest man in the company.

The author, S/Sgt Bill Henderson and company C forward observer, Lieutenant Terry Morrison.

Sgt John Carlevero from Cypress, TX was one of the finest soldiers to walk the jungles of South Vietnam. His specialty was rigging mechanical booby traps which protected our perimeters.

Steve Nyguard, Stretch Walker, Barney Congdon, Robert "Doc" Soltero and Gary Kiddy. Kiddy was awarded the bronze star w/valor for his action During a mortar attack.

Sgt Robert Blan from Oklahoma, Calvin Pulley from Carolina and "Brother" Span from New York. Span became a machine gunner for 2nd platoon.

At times C Co was convoyed to base camp from the helipads. Base camp was located near the ancient capitol of Hue. South Vietnam soldiers walk along highway QL1.

4

We were patrolling in the valleys around the hilltop called Firebase Brick when we were ordered to move onto the firebase to provide security support. Once we arrived, we were told General Sidney Berry, assistant commander of the 101st Airborne Division, would be sharing a Thanksgiving Day meal with a combat unit. That unit would be Second Platoon. I was quite excited, as I had met General Berry on the last day of ranger training at Eglin Air Force Base in Florida earlier in the year. He approached me in a manner that was not intimidating at all. He asked how the training was, how I felt it would benefit my upcoming experiences in VN, and then congratulated me on completion of the course. General Berry was a ranger graduate, signified by wearing the orange tab upon his left shoulder.

Before the general arrived, personnel had set up a tent on top of a bunker. The tent had two rows of tables and seating for about thirty people. After the general made his way to the tent, members of second platoon, along with Captain Newman, were seated. We were served Thanksgiving turkey with all the trimmings. A fantastic meal! It was my first hot meal since arriving in country seven months earlier. I was really amazed at the relaxed attitude of the general. He was considered "a soldier's general" by later press reports as the newspapers wrote about the young brigadier general who had the makings to rise to the top of the military ladder. General Berry later became commandant of West Point. Unfortunately, it was under his watch that a cheating scandal among the cadets was exposed. The scandal tarnished his career forever.

As we moved from day to day, our mission changed. At times, we are asked by HQ to stop and make landing zones for helicopters. We do that by blowing the huge trees with explosives. They send out the required TNT, det cord, and plastic explosives as needed.

This day we are on a narrow ridgeline with fifty- to seventy-five-foot trees on the east and west sides of the ridge and several on top. After looking the landscape over, we determine which trees need to be removed. It appears there are three or four trees on each side of the ridge and about that many on top. Upon removal of the trees, a chopper can make a swift beeline to the ridge, land, and take off again. All afternoon, Second Platoon rigged the trees with the plastic C-4 explosives. We ring-mained them together with the det cord, which looks like clothesline wire. Once we are finished placing the explosives strategically, noting which direction the trees should fall, we all step back several hundred feet and talk about what is going to happen. Correction, what should happen if we did the right calculation of explosives on each tree. Every last stick of explosive is now in place.

A volunteer grabs the electronic clicker attached to a blasting cap, which is attached to a large containment of C-4 stuck on a tree. "Fire in the hole" is repeated three times, and then a loud explosion occurs. We see trees toppling the way they were supposed to go. But hold on, the huge tree smack-dab in the center of the flyway did not go down! We stare in disbelief. The standing tree, now dangerously damaged but still upright, will prevent any helicopter from landing. My first thoughts are "We have no more explosives, we have a dangerous unstable tree that could fall in any direction, and this is the pickup site for our extraction." Everyone stays put while I walk to inspect the tree. There is a gaping hole torn from the side of the tree where the explosives were placed. I ringed this tree personally with Sergeant Carlevero. The two of us tied forty pounds of the plastic C-4, all that was remaining to the side of this tree. It is disappointing! It is dangerous as it still stands. I walk back to the others and ask, "Are you guys sure we have no more explosives?"

Before anyone could answer, a loud creaking sound came from the direction of the standing tree. We all looked on in disbelief and then relief as that huge hardwood giant slowly leaned to one side, then came crashing down. It was like, "We are out of here!" The smiles on their faces still make me smile today!

That was not our first experience blowing trees with plastic and TNT explosives. Plastic C-4 is much faster than TNT at about thirty-two thousand feet per second, and TNT is faster than dynamite, which is about twenty-two thousand feet per second. We did a job earlier using just TNT that came in one-pound blocks. The explosives were dropped off by helicopter. We had one case of fifty pounds that we did not use. That night, thinking it too dangerous to leave it within the perimeter of our defensive positions, I had two soldiers take it out and beyond and hide it among the foliage and brush. We will retrieve it tomorrow and then divide it up among us to carry. Next day, we got an order to move out quickly and forgot about the hidden explosives. No more was said about it.

About a month later, we walked onto a site that looked somewhat familiar. We prepared to set up an NDP. Sergeant Carlevero took his squad around the perimeter, out about 100' over the hill to check out possible enemy emplacements and signs that they were in the area. When he returned, he had that strange look on his face and said, "Ranger, you are not going to believe this! We found a box of TNT covered in some brush." Of course we both remembered and then confirmed, this was the same site we had been at earlier. So now what do we do? As John and I talked and thought about it, two things were clear. We did not want it to fall into enemy hands, and we did not want to detonate it, as it was sure to give away our location. If it was dynamite, we could rip open the paper rolls and scatter it to the wind. But this is TNT in blocks 2 × 2 × 2 inches in solid form. I grabbed a block and carefully started to break it into small pieces. I had the others stay far away as I did not know how stable it was when subject to pulverizing.

Seeing that this will work without detonating it, three or four of us began the task of breaking the explosive into small pieces. The best way was to empty the box, place several one-pound blocks back into the box, then use hard blunt sticks to pulverize the TNT. I was sure we did not want to use a rock or metal to pulverize as that might cause a spark and explosion. After four to five blocks were pulverized, we would empty the box by throwing the dust into the air. Thus we destroyed fifty pounds of TNT and learned that it could be neutralized in this manner.

We are on the trail, moving rapidly in the hot humid air. We have several new people with us who may not have properly acclimated to the climate. It was apparent the heat and dehydration was affecting many in the platoon. We stopped, and someone called out for Soltero, our medic. I walked back to where Doc was putting an IV into a young man. Two other soldiers were down a few yards away. I recognized one was Pully from one of the Carolinas. "Doc, we have two more down and not looking good," I holler out.

Doc shouts back to me, "Take my bag and get an IV into one of them."

"What do I do, never did it before," I shout back. So with the IV in hand, I prepare to work on Pully.

Doc shouts instructions, "Just find a vein, stick the needle in, and then attach the bottle of fluid."

"A bubble is forming under his skin," I tell Doc.

"You missed the vein, get the needle into the vein," Doc responds. After the third time, I find the vein and the fluid starts to enter Pully's body. Within thirty minutes, the helicopter has landed, and we begin transporting the fallen to the choppers.

Several days later, a helicopter lands, and Pully jumps out. I approach him and ask, "How are you doing, Pully?"

In that Carolina drawl, his says, "Oh I feel all right, but my arm is sure sore." I look at the arm that I stuck needles into, and it is all black and blue. We all grin as everyone heard about the difficult time I had sticking Pully with an IV.

We prepare to combat assault into an area that has been prepped with escorting cobra gunships. From the air, we can see that there are fires and smoke below. I'm thinking that maybe our LZ is on fire. "How will this work?" As our helicopter begins the descent, it is confirmed that the landing zone is filled with smoke and fire. The copter comes in at about ten feet from landing and then hovers; smoke is swirling all around. The door gunner taps me on the head. I look up, and he indicates that I should jump. I shake my head negative, pointing down, wanting the pilot to go lower. I look over my shoulder, and the others on the backside wait for me to jump. Again I shake my head no. We have full rucksacks. It's obvious the pilot wants us to bail out so he does not put his machine at risk near the fires on the ground. I'm thinking ten feet with seventy pounds on our backs, someone is going to get hurt! When the pilot saw that no one was jumping, he lifted quickly, straight up, and then made a sharp turn to come around again.

This second time around, the pilot hovered again at ten feet. This time, the pilot had given the door gunner orders to push me out, which he did. The door gunner grabbed me from the back of my ruck, and with little effort, I went flying. The others followed. As we hit the ground, I did a tuck and roll down off the hill. Fortunately, the ruck was still on my back, and I had not lost hold of my M-16. I scrambled to my feet eager to get away from the flames and smoke into a clearing below the LZ. There the six of us linked up and checked ourselves out for possible injury. Finding we were all okay, we joined the remaining members of the platoon. Apparently everyone else fared well as there were no reports of injury. "Were we the only ones that had to jump?" When I think back on the things like this happening that were dangerous, my only thoughts are "That's just the way it was!" To this day, it's hard to fathom, and surely in conversation with others without this experience, they may think, "No way, surely you exaggerate!"

Late that afternoon, we find defensible high ground for an NDP. We anticipate a possible probing or encounter by the enemy. I indicate to everyone that we should "dig in" tonight especially deep and wide. With three to four people in a position, we want a hole large enough for all of us to get down into if the attack comes. We dig. We set out our claymore mines in front of our positions and set up our guard watch rotations. I take last watch, and Larry T is on first watch. Barney and I lie prone on our backs on the ground behind the foxhole and try to sleep. Tonight I fall asleep quickly.

I am startled awake by a loud noise out in front of our position. I sit up immediately. At the same time, a loud explosive flash occurs right in front of the hole where Larry is on guard. I immediately feel a sharp impact and pain on my forehead. The flash of the explosion had reduced my night vision. Even though, I am still able to see Larry hunched down in the hole. As I put my hand to my head, I note it comes away bloody. Another noise out front, so I quickly lie back prone not wanting to take another hit before the anticipated explosion. After the next explosion, I crawled on my belly to Larry and say, "Larry, I'm hit!"

By this time, blood was running down my face somewhat blinding me as head injuries bleed profusely. I'm in the hole with Larry, and in the next explosive light, Larry sees my face. I'll never forget his words, "Oh my God!" Someone is throwing hand grenades, and they are exploding near us. We stay down low. Again I run my hand to my forehead and feel a fragment of metal stuck into my skull.

Barney is behind me, and I tell him to call LT that I'm hit and bleeding. LT says he will send Doc Soltero down to our position, but I say negative, "I'm coming up. I'll meet him halfway."

Explosions are still occurring out front as I crawl toward the command post. Doc meets me, and he sees that I may be close to going into shock. I laugh at his words when he says, "Do you want a cigarette?"

I respond, "Are you crazy, Doc?" Here we are out in the open! Doc is sitting upright on his knees, and I am prone on my back, trying to stay low. This guy is fearless! We all knew he was the best, and we counted on him to make us well in so many ways.

Doc looks at me and assesses that we need to call a medevac chopper tonight. I tell him no way. We both know how that would compromise everyone, including endangering the entire medevac crew. "Doc, just pull the fragment out and put a bandage on." The fragment was about the size of one's small fingernail. With my hand, I could feel the metal fragment protruding. I could tell it lodged well into my skull. Doc wrapped my head, and I crawled back to my position. By morning, I had a terrific headache. Doc made it known to me again he could not pull the fragment stuck in my forehead. I allowed LT to call the medevac to take me out.

A standard procedure here: If an attack occurs during the night, the last thing we do is fire our weapons. The muzzle flash gives away the position, allowing the enemy to know your exact location. Our first line of defense is the trip wire to illuminate enemy in the area. There were none out. In this case where I was injured by a fragmented grenade, it was thrown by one of our own but bounced back into my position when it hit a tree. We did not know that until morning that I was injured by "friendly fire."

It was very possible that the position next to ours was being probed by the enemy; thus, the soldier on guard reacted to what he thought was a threatening situation. But we did confirm that it was "Rubber Arm Galatich" that was throwing grenades during the night!

The trees were very tall; therefore, the helicopter called to pick me up had to hover above the treetops and send a penetrater down through the canopy. I had ridden a penetrater before during stateside training. I knew you had to let the cable touch the ground before grabbing on to it. The static electricity could knock you over. I climbed on, and they winched me up. I prayed all the way up and continued until we made elevation to where an RPG could not reach us. This was a dangerous time for all of us, helicopter crew and me. A single rock-propelled grenade (RPG) could cause the helicopter to crash, and I would be under it. I was winched in, and off we went to the aid station.

The doctors at base camp removed the fragment, bandaged the wound, and sent me on. I elected to stay in the rear area for two to three days until the wound showed signs of healing. I was concerned about the pressure of the steel helmet band, which lay directly over the wound when I placed it on my head. "In a few days, the pain will be gone, and I can wear the helmet," so I thought.

When I thought it was time to go out and join the platoon, I waited on the helipad for a time. Within an hour, my head was splitting with the most terrific headache. By the time I reached the others, I was almost blinded with the migraine headache. That night, I did not pull guard. I realized the pressure of the helmet aggravated the injury. The next day, I strapped the helmet to the back of my rucksack. Still, the headache persisted. Within a couple days, we walked onto Firebase Brick, and the head pain was so severe, I began vomiting. Again, the others pulled my guard duty.

When I had time, I stumbled down to the underground aid station and told the doctor my problem. I was disappointed in his reaction to my story. I remember the feeling he portrayed to me: "Just another soldier hoping to get out of the jungle." He gave me a bottle of aspirin and told me not to wear my helmet! I went back into the bunker on the perimeter and slept for what I remember to be almost two days with intermittent awakening. I remember being so thankful to the others that gave up their sleep so that I could heal.

5

After Captain Newman left the field to become the assistant commandant at the Screaming Eagle Replacement Center (SERTS), a new company commander joined us. He was Captain Whitmore. I did not learn much about his prior, but the first mission he led us on was in a lowlands assignment. We were ready—reaction force to replace other units that went in for a few days standdown. Therefore, we were replacing a company that worked in the lowlands contrary to our past experience in the mountain jungles.

LT was to remain behind on this mission. I received the operation order from the captain the night before and then went to the hooch where Second Platoon had been bunking the night before. That first night we returned from the field was one that was quite memorable for me. We were all together, twelve to fifteen of us who respected and enjoyed one another's company and together had experienced much in the jungle beyond. I felt a real close bond to these men. Someone brought in a couple cases of cold beer. We were able to get hot showers that evening. We got clean clothes. What more was there to ask? This was really living!

Sergeant Blan from Alva, Oklahoma, played a little country music on his tape deck. Then he sang the song "Oke from Muskogee." We all laughed, cheered, and jeered. It was a grand night of levity. George wanted to show us the reason for being on sick call—surgery on his hemorrhoids! We all declined the invitation to look! So it was that night that we all forgot the past and did not think of the tomorrow.

Earlier before the beer was consumed, I relayed the op order. It was simple yet a different mission. "We are to be trucked instead of riding helicopters to a destination outside a village. We are to leave in darkness so that we can be outside the village at first light. We will walk through the village and proceed beyond to a field of rice paddies, walking on the berm of the paddy. Once we leave the paddies, we will be in tall elephant grass and low shrubs. We shall exhibit all caution through the village and beyond as there will be civilians near," something that we were not accustomed to in the mountains.

This was a company-sized operation. Charlie Company was being transported in four trucks with seats on the sides and covered with tarp. We board in the dark. I crawled inside the cab beside the driver. I noticed this driver wanted to be right "in the tailpipe" of the truck in front. My immediate thought was, *Too close, an ambush or mine along the road would take out more than one truck and the men riding.* I made a comment about backing off a bit. He ignores my suggestion; in fact, he got even closer to the vehicle in front. I think he wanted me to know he was in charge of his truck. One more time I asked him to back off. He snapped back, "I'm driving this truck!" I had already noted his rank, and he was a specialist. I outranked him by several stripes, plus I had enough of his stupidity and insolence.

"Slow this —— truck down or I'm going to stop you right here in the middle of the [expletive] road. It's obvious you know nothing about ambushes. I'm responsible for these men in the back. You will not endanger their lives!" Now, if anyone has ever heard me speak loudly and forcefully, you know he got the message!

We dismounted the trucks, and at first light, we walk through the village. It was apparent the villagers had seen soldiers before. The little ones came out and spoke excitedly in Vietnamese. I don't know if our group looked friendly, as this was the first time that we had been around civilians. I sensed that the others felt as I did, "Let's get on through this village, away from what we don't know." Shortly the little ones followed us and shouted in English, "GI want soda?" Their presence was distracting to the men in the rear of the platoon. I observed that the children kept a close distance to the trailing members. An accident could happen quickly. Soon we will be looking for a place to stop and spend the evening in an NDP, and we don't want the children following. I walked back to the rear of the column and shouted "Dei Dei Mau" to the children, which means get away in French/Vietnamese. Now we are in scrub brush, and every sudden appearance of a villager is cause for a reflex action by our men. Once again, I walked back to the end of the column and shouted, "Dei Dei Mau!"

Just then a young girl, approximately eight to ten years old, suddenly stepped from behind a bush and shouted at me in perfect English, "You [expletive] lifer." She was white! She had red hair and was taller than the others! Just as quickly as she appeared, she darted behind the bush. I did the math later that day. She was about ten years old, and this was 1970. What was going on here in 1960? By the way, a *lifer* is a derogatory term that draftees give to career military men whom they do not like.

We move onward the next day away from the village. We are still in the lowlands with scrub brush and elephant grass. It's been raining almost every day. We come to a river that has doubled in size according my map. The three platoon leaders meet together with the captain, and he tells us that we are going to wade across as we have to be in a position tomorrow that warrants our being across the river. I estimate the river to be at least four hundred feet across, and it's flowing rapidly. We don't know how deep the water is, but I am convinced wading across with our ordinance is dangerous. He leads us into the water. The captain is a big man. I follow until the water gets to my chest. I see that we are nowhere near the other side to safety. I return to the riverbank and say, "We aren't going to do this." He comes back upon the bank to join us.

It's not my position as a subordinate to question the captain's decision, but this is Vietnam. I am an enlisted man with more experience than the captain. I have no qualms about telling this officer that he is wrong. I tell him, "It's too dangerous. We lost a man to drowning less than two months ago."

He replies, "Okay, have your men inflate their air mattresses." The rest of us looked at one another in disbelief. He's the only one with an air mattress! We sleep on the ground with nothing between us! Being this is his first mission, he has much to learn, and he must learn quickly.

The captain confers with headquarters, and apparently, he convinces personnel back in the rear that crossing the flooded waters cannot be done at this time. We move in a different direction parallel to the water. Tonight we set up in an NDP on flat level ground, there being no high ground in the lowlands. We are in the midst of scrub brush and trees, no taller than six feet in height. This is different from our experiences in the mountains bordering North Vietnam. I sense everyone is uneasy with this area of operation. We have a village a short distance away. The civilians know our location this evening. We dig in shallow fighting positions for each position and prepare to set out our early warning devices. Daylight is rapidly diminishing.

Where to protect our perimeter with so much indefensible ground? The short trees are everywhere, plus there appears to be so many avenues of approach the enemy could take to attack our positions. I spot a likely avenue, which is out beyond the position I will be in this night. As my RTO and two others set up the defensive night position, I walk to the outer perimeter to set up a trip wire to be attached to a white phosphorous grenade. I tie the grenade onto a small sapling approximately two inches in diameter. If I were an enemy soldier, I would approach this position through this avenue. I spot another small sapling about five feet away from the grenade. The wire, about two feet above the ground, will be stretched from this sapling to the grenade's pin. It's getting dark. I cannot see the men on the perimeter, but they know that I am out and beyond their position.

Now I have to work fast as it is almost total darkness. I stretch the attached wire across the open area and feel with my hands the location of the grenade, already attached to the tree. I want a hair trigger that will trip the grenade without tripping the advancing enemy when they hit the taut wire. I string the tripwire through the loop of the grenade pin and continue to pull the wire tight. I have my right hand above the two release points. I want the end of the pin to be just barely touching the outer secure orifice. With my right hand, I can feel the pin moving slightly as I pull the trip wire even tighter.

Suddenly there is a bright flash. White hot phosphorous is shooting directly into the air, illuminating everything nearby as the phosphorous is supposed to do. With my left hand, I had pulled the wire too tight, and the end of the grenade pin slipped out of the orifice, causing it to explode. My right hand was completely over the top of the grenade when it flared. My first impulse was to extinguish the flare's blinding brightness. These things happen occasionally over time. The men are supposed to place their steel helmet over the burning fire to stop the illumination. I couldn't do that as the flare was tied to the tree. Instinctively I drove my left foot down hard on top of the flare, ripping it from the tree. Just as it hit the ground, I gave it another stomp, and the flare miraculously went dark.

I know that I am burned severely on my right hand. Already the inside of my hand is one huge blister. Two fingers are fused together. In the darkness, I feel the burned skin and sense the extreme pain. White phosphorous continues to burn deep into the palm of my hand. But I am relieved that the illuminating flare is out! I walk back to the perimeter and tell LT, who had again recently joined us, that I am burned. Of course they saw the flare! The pain is excruciating! The medic is summoned, and I plead, "Do you have something for this?" He is new in the unit. Somehow our regular medic, Doc Soltero, was sent out with another unit. I needed, wanted Soltero! Doc was so competent that every fighting unit wanted Soltero!

By now I am barely able to remain quiet. The medic does not know what to do in this total darkness situation. I plead for morphine, knowing he has it in his bag. He reaches into the bag, pulls out a jar of salve, which he begins to apply on the burn. At this point, I just wanted anything, but the salve was totally wrong as it kept the burning heat in the hand. He wouldn't give me morphine. LT says he will call for a medevac, which I declined. Already our position may have been compromised. A medevac chopper would be extremely dangerous this evening for everyone, including the helicopter crew. "No. I will go out in the morning!"

The pain is blinding me. I go back to my position with the others. It's obvious I'm no good to anyone tonight. The others say they will pull my guard rotation. Just awful! I hurt so badly! The pain will not let up. I try to remain quiet, no sound, no moaning. Just bite down on something! All this is going through my head as I lay back on the ground. I try to sleep, hoping sleep will dull the pain. Then it hits me!

Years ago, I read about British soldiers in WWI and how they dressed their burns by pouring the tea from their canteens over their burns. "But I don't have tea in my canteen!" Nevertheless, I take out my canteen, poured water into the cup, and then I placed my hand in the liquid. Immediately, the relief was there! The cool water on the hand was better than anything imaginable. "Now maybe I can sleep!" Just as I think I'm okay, the water has been heated from the burn, and the severe pain strikes again. I tell the others what I am doing, and together they understand. When the water reaches that temperature causing the pain to return, they will dump it and add more water. I love these guys! And to this day, through my blinding pain, I cannot remember who was in my position with Barney. Through each guard rotation, they tend to my hand with freshwater. I slept fitfully. But as discussed, when the one on guard heard my moaning, the water in the cup was replaced.

At first light and with the outer perimeter secured, a medevac chopper came to take me in. As I waited for the chopper to land, I overheard LT say to the others, "This will be the last time that we see S/Sgt. Henderson." That comment made me feel so awful. I felt such a bond to these men, and I liked to think it was mutual. I knew the burn was significant and would need time to heal. I don't know what others were thinking, but I do know that loss of anyone in leadership is a blow to morale. We had served together, experiencing so much on a daily basis, much more than this account reveals. My pain had subsided, but the thought of going out like this was painful. This was my doing, my accident. No one else did this to me. My carelessness brought this upon all of us.

As expected, the hospital triage is right next to the helipad. Within fifteen minutes from time of pickup and landing, I am escorted to the operating area. The doctors are efficient. Within minutes, I am on my back on a table, and they are surveying the right hand. I hear one doctor say, "We have to clean the wound, remove the salve, and cut away the blisters." So it is again that the pain is so intense! I am literally yelling at the doctors about the pain as they wipe the salve from the burn. My right hand is clamped down, the left arm is held down by a strap. This is more pain than the night before! After removing the salve, they begin cutting away the blistered skin! So painful! No morphine! Nothing to dull the pain! What seemed like an hour, the wound was dressed, and I was sitting upright, exhausted, listening to the doctor tell how I should care for the burn. Every two days change the dressing, no water on the wound, and be aware of infection and so on. I knew about infection. They call it "jungle rot" in Vietnam.

I don't even know where I am in relation to my base camp even though I was here two months earlier with the head wound. I walk back into the med center, and I say, "You got some way to get me to my base camp?" I'm foggy. I still hurt. A young soldier directs me to a jeep, and I tell him my unit: C Company, 2nd 501st. He knows; he drives. I'm thinking, *He's transported others before this day!*

So it is that I spent time in the secure rear area, waiting for my hand to heal. As recommended by the doctors, the dressing is changed regularly at the aid station. I don't know my future. What does the army do with a soldier who is unable to perform his duty, especially an infantry trained soldier! I am in limbo.

I report to company headquarters each day and let them know my status. From there, I retreat to my tent where I have an army cot. I do more reading, sleeping, and writing letters. The cot is much better than on the ground! After about two weeks, I am told by the first sergeant that I need to report to the Screaming Eagle Replacement Center (SERTS) at camp Eagle north of this location. It appears that my former company commander, Captain Ray Newman, found out that I was out of the field recovering from burns, and he wanted me to come to SERTS. Captain Newman is now the assistant commandant at SERTS!

Knowing that my hand will heal in coming months, the military wants some productive work from me. When it looks like I can fulfill a slot in the replacement center, the army assigns me to a job that greets incoming soldiers to Vietnam. It is here that I meet Tom

McKinnon from North Dakota. Most of us from the Midwest have SS numbers that begin with 501 or 502. It was at this point that I noticed the new in-country recruit, Tom McKinnon, had a SS number as 501. The name McKinnon was the same as I had served with in basic training, only his name was Paul. "Do you know anyone by the name of Paul McKinnon?" I asked the new recruit who was standing in formation.

"Yes, Sarge, he is my brother," he replied. So it was that I met a fellow North Dakota native on my last days in Vietnam as he entered the country to begin his 364-day and 1-wake-up tour of duty in the Republic of South Vietnam.

Five years later, Tom McKinnon and I met again in Lisbon, North Dakota where both of us were employed as public school teachers until each of us retired from that profession. During our time as instructors we formed a house painting business and called ourselves Henderson McKinnon Painters. We worked together for over twenty years.

One day I am called to the office of Captain Newman. He tells me that Staff Sergeant Hughes is out of the field back at camp in Phu Bai. He is not getting along well. Hughes's constant drinking is getting him in trouble quite often. "I want to you to go down to Phu Bai and bring S/Sgt. Hughes back here," says the captain. I thought it an unusual directive since I have no paperwork for Hughes and the First Sergeant usually handles these things. Without questioning the captain, I go out to the chopper helipad and ask around for a ride to Phu Bai. "Anyone going south to Phu Bai today?" I keep asking the pilots. Finally, one indicates he is headed that way in a short time. I jump on, and soon we are in the air.

When I find S/Sgt. Hughes, he is a mess. He is still intoxicated from the day-night earlier. I tell him that I'm here to take him back to SERTS as directed by Captain Newman. "Captain Newman wants me at SERTS?" he asks. We both know the bond that the three of us had from our experiences in the bush. "Well, I'll be damned," Hughes replies.

We gather up his personal gear, grab the weapon assigned to him, and we walk out to the main gate just off highway QL1, the major north-south highway along the east coast of South Vietnam. The gate guard asks about our intentions. I tell him we are going north, and we are looking to hitch a ride on a truck going that direction. Within a short time, we load in the back of a deuce and a half (two-and-a-half-ton truck), and we begin the journey north. I look at S/Sgt. Hughes as the countryside rolls by. He has a smile on his face. He knows he is going to "another land" less hostile than the bush. I keep thinking, *I hope this works.* Captain Newman is out on a limb bringing Staff Sergeant Warren Allen Hughes to SERTS. I know what can happen!

Newman respected this "salty old dog," who always performed professionally in the field. I was impressed with Newman reaching out to save a friend from the harshness of the jungle. Surely Hughes would have been sent back out to the bush within a short time, as his antics could/would not be tolerated much longer. Can he survive at SERTS, even though the assistant commandant is a friend? Yes, events did occur with S/Sgt. Hughes. His drinking caused more than one ruckus on post.

My hand has nearly healed from the burn. There is less chance of infection. I no longer have to report to the aid station for new dressings. The bandages have been removed, but the new skin is very tender. My job at SERTS does not require any physical activity with my hands. I have a lot of time to read and reflect and write letters. I read the military publication *Stars and Stripes* each day. I listen to the military broadcast radio, which seems to be reporting about the ugly mood in America in regard to this war. I wonder what kind of experience I'll have when I set foot on US soil. I really don't care right now. I'm getting short, meaning just a few days left in country. S/Sgt. Hughes will be leaving with me. We will leave together, as we came to Vietnam on the same date.

6

I'm getting nervous. I've heard the stories about soldiers with just a few days remaining. These soldiers left country in a body bag. A mortar or rocket attack could occur anytime. Such a waste to die with days remaining! I have one more "wake-up"! S/Sgt. Hughes is ready to go. I don't see him the night before, but he looks reasonably well as we jump in a military jeep to take us to Phu Bai. From Phu Bai, we will board a C-130 to fly us to Danang. From Danang, we fly directly to Okinawa, Japan; then, a seventeen-hour flight to Seattle, Washington. We are back "in the world"!

We are in Danang being processed to leave South Vietnam. The person in charge of out- processing is not tolerant of anyone talking during his presentation. He wants strict attention from everyone, including S/Sgt. Hughes, who found a source for alcohol, and he is intoxicated.

He is constantly talking in that loud gravelly voice. Hughes ignores the threats by the presenter who tells him that he will be held over and will miss this flight home if he does not contain himself. Hughes babbles on. Finally, the presenter calls for the MPs to have S/Sgt. Hughes removed from the room. There are several hundreds of us in that room. Everyone is wondering, "What is wrong with this guy? Does he not want to go home?" I know Hughes; this was expected if he got his hands on a bottle. S/Sgt. Hughes leaves with the military police, and I'm thinking, *I won't see Staff Sergeant Warren Allen Hughes again.*

Wrong! As we board the airplane, I hear a familiar voice, "S/Sgt. Henderson, back here! I saved you a seat." Sure enough there was Hughes sitting in the last row back of the plane. According to Hughes, the MPs took him to the loading dock and had him load duffle bags onto the plane. Then they put him in the most uncomfortable seat in the airplane for the long seventeen-hour flight home. These seats were always upright, never able to lean back as the wall was tight against the seat. And he saved a seat for me! He grinned broadly as I thanked him for his consideration.

As the plane taxied down the runway, the din of excited military voices filled the air. When the wheels lifted from the tarmac, there was a loud shout of hoorays. This was the moment we had all waited for, the moment when it was unimaginable one year ago. Many of us had our doubts about surviving in Vietnam, especially those of us who were assigned infantry. The emotion at that time was overwhelming! You could see it in the faces on all who were aboard. "Now we have to get up into a safe altitude."

And it was at that time the plane shuttered! And just like that, we were all quiet. "No, don't let this plane fall from the sky," I reacted in a quick prayer. Within seconds, the plane smoothed out into its steady climb over the Pacific Ocean. As we relaxed, the conversation again became jovial but much more subdued than during takeoff. We are on our way home! One more refueling stop in Okinawa, then onward again, straight across the Pacific with a tailwind. We won't be taking the great circle route to Alaska and south as the westerly winds are in our favor going east.

We land at SeaTac International Airport and are directed off the plane. I note small gatherings of civilians along the fences just beyond the restricted areas. We do not walk in the covered walkways that you see at airports today. We are dismounting outside and must pass by the people lining the restricted fences. There are loud, boisterous, demeaning shouts from some of these onlookers. "Baby killers! How many did you kill? Shame, shame!"

We are loaded into a military bus and taken directly to Fort Lewis military base. Here we are debriefed for a period of about thirty minutes, then sent to comfortable quarters nearby. We shower and put on a clean uniform. This is the same uniform that I wore before shipping overseas. They saved it for me, even had it pressed!

We are told there will be a steak dinner tonight for those of us who are mustering out of the military permanently. It is this night that we sit four at a table and we enjoy a glass of wine or a beer with the meal that is about to be served. In the center of the table, a candle is burning! The only thing missing is my dinner date! I sit back and take in the surroundings. I never want this moment to end! The waiters are scurrying around with water glasses and bringing the steak dinners from the kitchen. It is quiet in the room. We are all just mesmerized by the comfort, the smells, and the attentiveness of the waiters and the calming atmosphere of the dining room.

For me, I am cleaned up. I no longer wear the jungle fatigues! I take a moment to thank God for bringing me to this time in my life. It seemed like years before this date and an entire lifetime. So much had happened in that span of time. My thoughts kept drifting back to various moments in the jungles of South Vietnam. Is this real? I pause to think about the thousands of soldiers who were unable to return to this setting. I recall the monsoon season and how terribly wet and cold we were for days at a time. I recall historical events where the soldiers of previous wars suffered so dearly. All these thoughts kept racing through my head. But now, I just want to cast the darkest memories aside and enjoy this moment! Thank God for life!

I am free to leave the next morning. My plan is to travel to Eugene, Oregon, to visit a friend. I will spend two nights there before continuing on to Bismarck, North Dakota. I arrive in Eugene unannounced without prior notification to the friend whom I will see that evening. Everything I do now is not the "hurry" that I had experienced in the past. I want to take in every moment! When my plane lands in Eugene, I walk into the airport lounge and order a beer. It is a small airport, and the lounge is empty. I will decide when to call and where to go later. I just want to take in this moment. The club manager and I make small talk.

He is friendly! I spot an empty pool table. I'm reminded about all the pool I used to play in earlier life. I walk over to the table and pick up a cue. The bartender-manager and I rack the balls for a game of eight ball.

Just as I am about to break, four young men walk into the lounge. I'm wearing my class A uniform that they note. Immediately the group takes on a derisive attitude with their words directed at me. I assume they are college students out on the night! I ignore their words. They continue. I break the rack, then turn quickly with the cue stick in a defensive-offensive position, not knowing if they want this to escalate. The heavy end of the cue is now my weapon. Immediately the manager jumps between us and tells the group to leave. It is over, but it was my first experience in a close encounter with the ugly mood of an American public!

I meet and greet my friend and divulge my plans. Two days here, and then I must move on. My friend is an excellent host. The first day, the plan is to go to the coast and dig for clams along the shore. That was a new experience and delightful. That night, we are meeting friends and friends of friends at a nightclub. I put on my civilian clothes, not wanting to draw attention inviting another encounter. There is much laughter and levity and much talk about the songs that are playing. There is talk about the popular artists in music, popular movies, what is happening on campus, in the city. They all seem to know what is going on in this part of "the world." I know not what they speak about. All I can think about is the life and friends I left in Vietnam three days ago. My mind is not in the present. In fact, I feel so disconnected I want to run away from this gathering. Where do I go? I get up and walk outside. My friend follows and asks, "Is something wrong? Did I do, say something to upset you?"

"No, no," I respond. "It isn't you, it's me." And I cannot tell her because I do not know the answer to my troubled self. Was it the noise in the room, just faces that had no meaning to me? The laughter was like screams coming out of the mouths of the women. The men looked so pathetic in their attempt to impress the ladies. "I guess I'm not ready for this. I need to go back to the apartment," I say somewhat apologetically.

The next day, I board a plane for North Dakota. We are required to fly in uniform in order to get the military rate. As I enter the airplane, the stewardess gives me the most hateful look. She does not greet me. I know the look of contempt. I continue down the aisle until I find my seat. I sit by the window, and soon thereafter a middle-aged gentleman sits next to me. He is friendly! He engages me in conversation, and I immediately know that I like this man and his attitude. He tells me he is a pastor at a church somewhere in the Midwest. Our next stop will be Billings, Montana. Then Bismarck, North Dakota. As was customary at that time, the airline industry served one free meal during flight. It was time to receive the meals from the stewardess. I heard the conversation among the passengers as they were asked about their preferences.

The same stewardess that looked so hateful while boarding asked my companion what he wanted to eat. He ordered. Then she looked at me and said, "I'm sorry, sir, but we are short on meals for this flight. I don't have anything for you. Since you are flying standby, surely you understand." I looked at her in disbelief! I pushed my tray upward and turned to the window. My seat companion touched me on the arm and said, "I can't eat this. You eat the sandwich."

"No," I replied. "It's yours." I'm still not able to turn from the window. Again he says to me, "I will send it back unless you agree to share it with me." This is an offer of kindness at a most hateful time by the stewardess.

I respond, "Of course, and I thank you for sharing. I don't want you to miss your meal."

Much later, I think about this and the earlier events. "How could this have happened to me, to us? I, and others returning from Vietnam, had just put our lives on line, for this?" The anger made my stomach churn. I thought about the fearful times, the physically trying times that we experienced because of the heat. I remembered Oscar unable to walk without pain, Larry and Steve constantly fighting the jungle rot on their arms. Harvel dead from drowning, the young medic killed after just a few weeks in Vietnam, the hundreds wounded and killed on and around Firebase Ripcord. My thoughts flashed back to the monsoons wet and cold, weeks at a time. I recalled the wounded and dead that we personally placed on the medevac choppers during the siege of Ripcord. I think about Doc Soltero, Labruna, Steve, Swantek, Punky, LT, and Larry. How were they received? How will they react to coming home to this America? They deserve better treatment than this!

Nearly one year ago I left the Bismarck airport relishing a farewell kiss and hug from a lovely young woman who found it in her heart to make this soldier happy. Now I am returning, and the thought of reuniting with family and friends becomes overwhelming. As I step down from the airplane, I see my brother Dale and my dad waiting outside to welcome and take me home. My mother did not make the three-hour trip from Scranton. I will greet her this evening. God is *good*!

As I wait to pick up my duffle bag, I'm just overwhelmed with emotion. I don't want this moment to end. Every moment is special, every moment is life that needs to be taken in and absorbed into my body. It was a lifetime past that I walked this airport building. Is this for real? The good and gracious God that I spent so much time talking with over the past two years has brought me back to this day, this day with family in familiar surroundings. "I love this moment! Thank you, Lord!"

I spend the next month in my hometown. I reacquainted with old friends and family. But there is an unsettling pall over myself. The war is still ongoing. I listen to all the news, broadcasts, and opinions on major networks. I sense firsthand the mood of America with this war in Vietnam. During my absence, the lottery was instilled. College students, who were deferred because of their enrollments, are now free to drop out without fear of being drafted.

My thoughts are always on Vietnam. Different smells and sights trigger thoughts from the past. The sounds of the day constantly bring me back to Vietnam. Day and night I relive each incident that had occurred. I become very restless. I want to leave the comfort of the farmhouse where I was raised as a child and go into the city. Once I am in the little city of Scranton, I feel I must leave immediately! "Where do I go? When will this overwhelming desire to keep moving allow me peace of mind?"

I began consuming large amounts of alcohol on a daily basis. I knew this to be wrong, and it scared me that I could hurt others when I had consumed too much. I knew the effects of alcohol on families, as my father abused alcohol quite frequently. All seven children witnessed troubling events following his abusive drinking. And so it was that I began making plans to travel, to leave this environment.

My good friend Les Schaefer agreed to travel with me. For the next three months, we traveled southward into Arizona, Mexico, California, then northward into Oregon, Washington, Idaho, and back to North Dakota through Montana. It was a journey that provided a diversion from the thoughts of Vietnam, thoughts that constantly bombarded my mind.

For years Vietnam was constantly on my mind, a regular flashback. "When will this torment end?" One evening after a weekend of drinking, a friend found me lying in the snow in my backyard. Is this how it ends, frozen in a snow bank?

In the northern climates, this is always a possibility for those who abuse alcohol. I knew I was in trouble. I resolved then to never let that happen again! I also recalled the pain and anguish in the family caused by my father's abusive drinking.

And then, miraculously a lifeline appeared out of nowhere. I received a telephone call from LT Carpenter, "a voice from the past," twelve years after Vietnam! A reunion of Second Platoon was being planned in Minneapolis for that summer. Could I make it? So it was that ten of us were able to meet and tell our stories and relive the moments we shared as a combat unit. After three days of talking and listening, in the presence of my wife who learned so much from the others, I felt an enormous weight lifted from my shoulders. Understandably, some of these past recollections shared, we found were perceived differently by members of this group.

After this first reunion of Second Platoon, I thought less frequently about my experiences in Vietnam. A sense of calm began to enter into my head. I realized this was a stabilizing event in my life. I thank God that I was able to link up once again with this fine group of men. Without a doubt, we still possess that brotherhood of camaraderie brought on by shared difficult times. I love those guys! I continue to communicate with them, having traveled three times to join the others in renewing the friendships that were bonded in the mountain jungles of South Vietnam! God is *good*! Life is *precious*! "Welcome home, Vietnam veterans!"

WILLIAM HENDERSON

Give Us Just a Bit More Time

It had been a long and distant flight from Cam Ranh Bay,
And when the big bird landed,
We were there to kiss the good Ole USA.

In the world is where it's happening,
The war in Nam a forgotten past.

We survived Cong's booby traps and shells,
And in just a matter of time
We were back upon the streets,
Chasing the good ole times.

Understand, we'd been gone for quite some time
And there was some living to catch upon!

"How was it," you asked?
As we searched for words to respond,
You replied, the Orioles won it all
While you were gone.

But of course, we couldn't relate one year's time
In just a few minutes of your precious time.

"Let us in your midst," we cried.
Been gone for just awhile!
Let us be like you, dear friends,
But give us just a bit more time.

"Were you scared," you asked?
By the way, we won the conference while you were away.
You shouldn't have been there anyway,
Is what the papers always say.

WALKING IN THE SHADOW OF DEATH

You did your best to make us feel that we should agree,
AND we want to be like you again,
Only … Give us a bit more time.

And now, we recall the landing of the plane
And in our joy upon returning then,
We forgot those upon the ground were chanting
Ho Chi Minh!

We want to be like you again,
Our friends;
But please … Give us just a bit more time.

Bill Henderson
1971

ABOUT THE AUTHOR

William Henderson served in the US military during the years 1969–71, having volunteered for the draft. He attended Noncommissioned Officer School and completed the elite ranger course at Fort Benning, Georgia. Henderson was awarded the coveted ranger tab upon successful completion of the program. His first mission in Vietnam was to lead his platoon in support of the beleaguered Firebase Ripcord. As a graduate of Dickinson State University, having majored in elementary education, William taught in a rural community prior to his service. He retired from teaching after thirty-two years in the classroom. The most important aspect of William's life is his love of family, love of country, and love of God.

CPSIA information can be obtained
at www.ICGtesting.com
Printed in the USA
LVHW090818031218
599057LV00009B/542/P

9 781640 031739